LONDON R

Brighton's First Suburb

CW00740118

**Dedicated to the memory of Rosemary Fittock,
a valued member of the
London Road Social History Group.**

Contents

An aeroplane view of London Road c1907 looking north
St. Bartholomew's church dominates the western skyline

London Road looking North c1905. Queen's Place and the Prince of Wales pub
are on the right and J. Sainsbury on the left

Brighton's First Suburb

… A person taking a walk along the main valley in 1800 would pass a few small houses in North Row (now Marlborough Place) and find himself in the open Downlands. Immediately in front, he would see the green Roundhill dominating the scene, whilst on the east were the steep slopes of Hilly Laine and the adjoining Sheep Down … Highways ran at the foot of the hills on each side, with open, rough, grassy flats inbetween (later known as North Steines and Levels), which in the winter months became marshes.

… A centre track hereabouts (now occupied by the Fountain) cut through the grassy south level on which St. Peter's Church now stands, and followed a straight line up the hill and over the Downs to Ditchling. In the widened part was situate (sic) a large area of low lying ground, known as the North Level. Between this North Level (edged by Ditchling Road) and the London Road, there was a slightly raised dryer piece of land in the shape of an elongated triangle. Centuries before, it had been used as a ground for the practice of archery, and, in the terrier Map of 1738, was thus known as the 'North Butts'. At the apex of this triangular piece of land was an inn, known as 'The Nag's Head' which at that time had an open southern aspect to the sea. This inn was a well-known coach house, and was solely used by the stage wagoners from London for the conveyance and the unloading of merchandise and goods. The distance from London was thus reckoned from this inn, and today one may see an iron plate, 'Brighton to London, 52miles,' fixed in the foot of the wall of the 'Prince of Wales' Inn close by the site. Stables and warehouses adjoined the inn to the north, and it was here that the little suburb became to be built, in the latter part of the eighteenth century, consisting of Brunswick Row & Court and a part of Oxford Street. … (The) houses are low and faced with cobbles, having red tiled roofs, with the front door opening into the living room. Some of the courts are but a few feet wide and paved, with a gutter-way running along the centre.

The large North Level, as open common, which came in very handy for the dwellers of these cottages during the summer months, serving as grazing ground for cows, sheep and horses, besides being a place for props and used as a drying ground for their laundry. … A plucky builder named George Marshall, built a row of similar small houses at the top of the meadow (now occupied by the Open Market). These houses started from the blacksmith's shop which stood a little way back from London Road. …With the advent of the railway, goods were no longer carried by stage waggoners, so that 'Ichabod' (The glory is departed) came to be written over the portals of 'The Nag's Head'. It was rebuilt and modernized in the middle of the last century, but its original usefulness had long since passed.

… For over a century, what with the erection of larger houses on all sides, these little cottages by 'The Nag's Head' have been hidden, but most of them still remain as they were built, and I venture to think, can lay claim to be known as 'Brighton's first suburb.

F.G.S Bramwell - Brighton & Hove Herald 31st March 1928 page 10

London Road c1907 from Cheapside looking north
The large private houses and gardens on the left have all been converted to shops

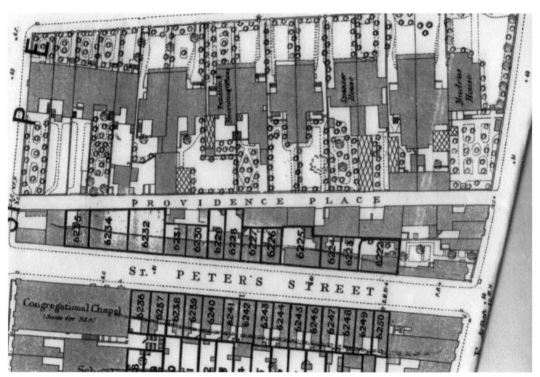

Ordnance Survey Map 1876 showing Nos. 1-17 London Road with their large front and back gardens.
Providence Place and St. Peter's Street are behind

London Road: A Timeline

If there is one theme that is fairly constant in the history and development of the London Road area from around 1750 to the present day, then it is the impact of change. Up to 1750, the area had probably seen only a modicum of change over a considerable period of history. The London Road valley was a dry valley through the chalk downs, formed by the action of water during a highly pluvial period in and after the Quaternary geological era. As the water table was high for many centuries it was a marshy area surrounded by farmland, downland pasture given over to sheep. However as Brighton gradually expanded, more of the land would have been used for arable farming with particular attention being given to vegetable and fruit provision. Furthermore, in undertaking this change, relatively large farm units would have been subdivided into fields and strips and leased out to tenants. But, in 1750 all this was to change.

1750: Development of the North Butts suburb, Queen's Place, Marshall's Row area.

1800-1825: Large houses built in Queen's Road, later renamed London Road. More development in the North Butts area along Oxford Street, Oxford Court, Brunswick Place North (Ditchling Road) and the use of London Road as the main route to and from London. Hanover Crescent built, along with St. Peter's Church.

1850-60: The arrival of the railway. Development of the railway workers' housing and locomotive works between London Road and the station.

1860-1870: Transport routes begin to evolve to Preston, Patcham and into the urban development of the Stanford estate north of Preston Circus. Early tram proposals are made. Some significant buildings developed e.g. St. Bartholomew's church.

1900: London Road develops as a shopping street, the tram system starts in the area and some demolition occurs around Preston Circus, which takes on the role of a major route interchange. The use of the housing in London Road by the 'gentility' starts to decline as the road becomes the main route into town and the transfer to commerce accelerates.

1904-1905: Large scale clearance of streets adjoining the station in order to extend the goods yard. Peel Street, Queen's Street and Fleet Street disappear. Final development of the tram routes in the area.

1915-1926: The Open Market is started in Oxford Street by ex-servicemen. This results in a battle for survival, first in Oxford St., then the Level and finally Marshall's Row.

1930s: Establishment of many national branded shops in the area e.g. Marks & Spencer, Brighton Co-op and smaller concerns like Home & Colonial and Lipton's. There are more clearances of old dwellings in Oxford Court, Marshall's Row and Francis Street. Trolleybuses replace trams in 1939 and during the war bombs destroy houses in Elder Place and Rose Hill Terrace. Prefabs appear in Viaduct Road and Rose Hill Terrace in 1944.

1950s: London Road shopping centre reaches the zenith of its importance. Plans are made to clear the houses in the working class hinterland between London Road and the Station.

1955-1965: The locomotive works closes in 1957. This had been a major source of employment in the town. Many streets from New England Road to Trafalgar Street are demolished. Trolleybuses disappear from the streets and the Open Market is rebuilt. The shopping area is under threat as plans materialise for Churchill Square. The prefabs are demolished and New England House is erected in New England Street.

1975-1985: As Churchill Square dominates Brighton's shopping scene, London Road declines. Marks & Spencer closes and Bellman's and Rosling's follow. Many smaller food stores give way to supermarkets. The Open Market starts to struggle and London Road is surrounded by dereliction.

1990s: Many plans are developed to bring life to the area. A major shopping complex from the Station down to the west side of London Road, incorporating St. Bartholomew's church in a piazza style square is proposed but defeated by councillors keen to protect the refurbishment of Churchill Square. A lorry park is proposed for the area and industrial buildings are erected behind London Road. Traffic congestion is a major problem and a traffic management scheme involving bus lanes and a one way system is implemented in two stages.

2000: The new millennium starts with controversy over plans for developing the old goods yard site from the station down to New England Street. Eventually plans are accepted for a mix of housing, hotels, offices and educational buildings.

2010: A new era of prosperity starts? Time will tell.

Agriculture to Industry and Commerce

Brighton's Street pattern in the 21st century is still heavily influenced by its ancient field system, this consisted of five open fields called 'laines' that surrounded the Old Town on all its landward sides. These fields were split into 'furlongs', which were bundles of largely parallel field strips called 'paulpieces' that were a legacy of the area's Anglo Saxon farming system. The north side of Brighton, including the London Road area, developed the distinctive street pattern it still possesses, as a direct result of this piecemeal pattern of landholding. This pattern can be clearly seen by comparing the streets in North Butts which all ran E-W with the streets across London Road in the Short Furlong which are aligned N-S, a direct reflection of the earlier strip field maps or 'terriers'.

Until the early 19th century an area of arable land on the northern fringe of the original parish of Brighton, was largely located in two furlongs out of the ten that comprised the North Laine, one of Brighton's five large open fields. These furlongs are the North Butts in the southern part of the area and The Crook that occupies the northern half. There is a line of housing (latterly shops) along the western edge of the area that form the eastern fringe of other North Laine furlongs, the Short or Fifth Furlong in the South and Crooked Furlong and Rottingdean Hedge Furlong in the north (See 1792 Map). A small area of Preston parish is where the Duke of York's cinema and Fire Station are located. To the east the Level which adjoins the North Laine, part of the manorial 'wastes' of the town is included and the line of buildings adjacent to this on the north – Park Crescent, and on the east Hanover Crescent and Richmond Place.

The earliest development in this area is on the north side of the Crook, where the Hare and Hounds pub was built as a traveller's rest on the Brighton – Preston borders. A date of 1795 has been ascribed to the original pub. This may be a clue to the unresolved issue of how old is London Road? It is not as old as is imagined. The old road into the resort from London came along the Dyke Road ridge past St. Nicholas Church and down North Street. Possibly this was owing to the Wellsbourne stream that flowed down the main valley from Patcham to Pool Valley that might have made the direct route less favourable.

The next phase was a speculative development in 1815 by the Duke of Dorset, the area's main landowner who held most of North Butts. His scheme was to build along the south and east fringes as terraced up-market housing, more modest housing along the western edge with the central area as small dwellings, yards and industrial activities. Until the 1840's there were still bricks being made in the Ditchling Road area. This must have presented a curious appearance to travellers into the resort, as this development was isolated from the built up area for about ten years

The growth of Brighton in the 1820s was among the most rapid in the country and the middle classes sought to escape the congested, cramped streets of central Brighton. With the seafront east and west of the Old Town given to higher class housing projects such as Regency Square and Kemp Town, the middle classes were catered for by new housing snaking out along the central valley to form terraces such as Grand Parade and Gloucester Place. Documentation is sketchy but the housing between Cheapside and Ann Street seems to be in place by 1825 and other buildings including the old vicarage by 1830. Maps of this period indicate that the built up area was continuous to the Preston parish border soon after 1830.

The 1st Sussex Volunteers march north along London Road
past the Northern Hotel and Cheapside in June 1907

F. W. Woolworth on the corner of Cheapside & London Road in 1965
Originally the site of a private residence called Madras House

On the east side of the North Butts, along Brunswick Place North at Adelphi Terrace and Prospect Place (now St. Peter's Place) the fine parades of terraced housing were in place by 1825 and development ran alongside both sides of the Level in a similar 'ribbon development' pattern. Slightly later the failure of the Ireland's Gardens scheme to the north of the Level enables work to start on Park Crescent.

A complete list of occupants of the housing exists for 1834 which helps to illustrate the social standing of the area. Many of these early occupants and owners were traders from the Old Town, men such as J.B. Phillipson, a chemist of St. James' Street, James Cordy, a wine merchant – both Town Commissioners – and Samuel Akehurst, a pastry cook and land owner and with Cordy a former High Constable of Brighton. Akehurst, Phillipson and George Augustus Riddlestorffer (furrier and lace warehouse), all had businesses in St. James' Street and the move over a mile to London Road probably illustrates the constraints on residential choice.

In the 1850s the social pattern changes and the London Road district takes on a more urban feel especially with the growth of the retail sector. The growth of the railway yards and workshops on the west of the North Butts area caused an expansion of working class railway housing in that area. By the 1860s over half the listed occupants were females, but still with trade as a substantial element. Two celebrated residents at this time were the umbrella maker Thomas Lulham and Arthur Hawker Cox of Cox's Pill Factory fame. At this time the social standing of London Road was in the balance when a soap and tallow works opened 400 yards away in Station Street and the presence of the railway works encouraged the dispersal of the middle class occupants. By 1886 Nos. 5 & 6 appear in directories as furniture dealers and from then on there is a steady increase in the number of retail outlets in the area. The final residences are shown clearly with walled front gardens in a photo of 1903.

The Twentieth Century

By the early 20th century the industrial picture had a duality with the heavy industry in the west around the railway and smaller enterprises located in the North Butts; slaughter yards, the blacksmith and a mineral water manufacturer. To the north across the border in Preston the Duke of York's Picture House was opened in 1910, replacing Longhurst's Brewery, catering for what was by then a densely populated area. Commerce was still dominated by local traders, in 1905; J. Sainsbury had arrived at 3, London Road.

With the growth of the northern suburbs, all this was to change. The period up to and after the First World War, saw a steady amalgamation of businesses, especially of the numerous drapers and outfitters. Nos. 1 & 2 London Road, The Crystal Palace Bazaar Co., was acquired by F. W. Woolworth and W. S. Hopson, milliners and drapers, became Ashdown & White, drapers, so adding to No. 6 to 7 & 8. This shop, together with No. 5, in turn became a new purpose-built Marks & Spencer in 1935. Marks & Spencer had started at the site of the present Superdrug in 1932, formerly the Jollyboy's department store. The Brighton Co-op moved out of North Road and by 1929 had a major investment with a huge shop in the Crook furlong. Branches of Woolworth, Boots, Timothy Whites and Taylor's, Lipton's, World's Stores and another Sainsbury's all appeared and local furnishers Cobbs had a new store built further north near Preston Circus. The Open Market was then relocated in the old cottages and gardens area of Marshall's Row.

W.S. Hopson, milliner & draper at Nos. 7 & 8 London Road c1907

After the Second World War there were changes to the area's appearance. Woolworths moved north to the old Rosling's store, their old shop being refurbished into a Sainsbury's supermarket. Marks & Spencer expanded, the locally owned Bellman's store

was taken over by Fine Fair and the Open Market was rebuilt. The shops were then sustained by the consumer boom of the 1950s but clearance schemes to the west of London Road caused a decrease in the local population and left rubble-strewn car parks and small industrial units.

After a slump in the early 70s, there was a brief recovery but this was short lived and by the 1980s London Road was once again losing trade. A major blow was the closure in 1986 of Marks & Spencer, which seemed to precipitate the area into an inner city feeling district of charity shops and 'Pound Stores' with the ever present fast food outlets. The recent loss of major stores, such as Woolworth and the Co-op, has hastened its decline.

A delightful comparison of London Road district of forty years ago, when private houses and long gardens were the general rule, with the thriving business centre of today, was made by the Mayor of Brighton (Councillor J Lord Thompson) at the third annual dinner of the London Road District Trader's Association … His Worship genially recalled how the traders of twenty years ago 'screamed' when the trams were started, fearing that the trams would take all their trade straight into town. But, as a matter of fact, the trams bring multitudes of people from the hilltops to London Road itself, and now, particularly on Fridays and Saturdays, the thoroughfare is a marvellous site, with great crowds of people shopping … The President said he had great admiration for those men who first opened shops in London Road, and who foresaw the great possibilities of the district as a trading centre. It is only thirty or thirty-five years ago that there was hardly a shop at all, but those men had the pluck to build, and to bring out shops over gardens onto the main road.

Rosling's stores c1932 just before the creation of the new store

The Gem Electric Theatre at 36a London Road opened in 1910 but closed in 1914.
It is now the site of Sussex Stationers plc.

GENERAL & FANCY DRAPERS
LACE CURTAIN SPECIALISTS

10   JENNER & COMP.�Y   10

HORROCKSES
LONGCLOTHS
FLANNELETTES
SHEETINGS &c

DIRECT
FROM THEIR
MILLS

IRISH
LINENS
DAMASKS
TOWELS &c

DIRECT
FROM
BELFAST

CURTAINS
direct from
NOTTINGHAM

JENNER & Cᵒ.

JENNER & Cᵒ. GE

'Those who are alive today have reaped the reward of their labours – and some of us have come in for the benefit!'

Brighton Herald 23rd January 1926

There were two Sainsbury's shops; one next to Woolworths, when it was on the corner of Cheapside, and the other one just beyond York Hill. They were the old style shops with the office desk at the end with a clock over the top, with different marble counters for each department like butter and bacon. There used to be racks of rabbits and chickens hanging up. They also had big baskets of eggs outside filled with eggs and they were ten or twelve for ten pence or a shilling according to size. I was the oldest of four children, so I was given the paper bag with the eggs to carry home. Beyond the York Hill Sainsbury's there were two butcher's shops and they would auction their meat. The butchers didn't have fridges then just big ice rooms with large squares of ice. They tried to clear the meat on Saturday, so that it would all be fresh meat the following week. The windows of the shops would open up and you could see the meat on the slabs and they would call out 'Half a crown for a shoulder of lamb and a chop for the old man's tea.' That went down well. People used to wear six months of black clothing and then go into grey and there was only one shop that sold mourning clothes. I remember going there after my grandmother died. There was also a 'Guinea' shop near Roslings (later Woolworth's) that sold ladies clothes. Dresses cost half a guinea (10/6d) and coats a guinea (£1.1s) but that was more late 30s and during the war.

At the bottom of Trafalgar Street there was a grocer's shop called Eltenton's. It used to fascinate me because of the sacks all around the wall containing brown sugar, split peas and beans. Whatever you wanted they would shovel it up into a blue bag and weigh it.

Doris Vaughan

London Road was a fine shopping area in the 1930s. There was the Co-op, Pocock's drapers, Marks & Spencer and Bellman's. As a youngster I was in Bellman's one day when Max Miller was opening a section and he put on quite an act.

Marie Benfield

My mother shopped in London Road. In those days it was a hive of industry and equally as popular as Western Road. At Christmas the whole street from Preston Circus to St. Peter's church was lit up with lights and decorations. You never saw a shop window that wasn't lit up. I remember Osborne's the grocers, which had marble counters and in front there were tins with press down lids with broken biscuits. It was rare that we ever had a proper biscuit. Mum also shopped at Woolworth's on the corner of Cheapside and London Road. The first thing you would be greeted with was the cake counter and mum used to buy a big thick cake with icing and marzipan on it.

David Huggins

I was ten when we moved to York Place opposite St. Peter's church. We lived above a tailor's shop near Potter's gentlemen's outfitters and Maynard's sweet shop. It was a very spacious flat for just three of us with two floors and an attic. We had quite a big back garden with a natural shelter down some steps. We took all our treasures there for safety during the war, including a beautiful antique gramophone but the shelter was bombed and we lost everything.

I went to the Intermediate school which was a very good school and I had a marvellous education there.

In the 1930s London Road was a very good shopping area. My parents knew Sydney Bellman who stated his shop Bellman's in Oxford Street and then moved to a larger shop in London Road. My father worked at Cobb's furniture store and he was a volunteer fireman. He used to buy his newspaper from a little newsagent in Ann Street and sadly the owner was machine-gunned during the war.

Pearl Lawrence

There was a shop on the corner of Trafalgar Street and York Place called Eltenton's grocers. They used to hang, rather foolishly we thought, hocks of bacon outside on the fascia board. About four of us would come tearing down Trafalgar Street on our bikes like Bengal Lancers. We'd be carrying poles with funny hooks on for pulling down shop blinds and we'd hook the bacon off the fascia and ride round the corner into London Road and get away. I can tell you that not many parents took the hock of bacon back – not in those days.

There was an old lady who sold matches at the bottom of Ann Street just outside Mears the greengrocers. She had a little notice down the front that fitted round her waist and went down to her ankles saying 'Due to circumstances beyond my control I'm forced to stand here and sell these things' and then something saying she was blind.

Gordon Dean

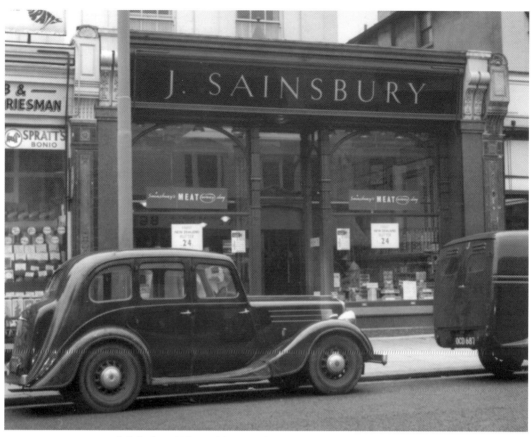

J. Sainsbury Ltd. provision merchants at 55 London Road c1955
The shop was opened in 1925 and closed in 1969. It is now the site of Betfred

London Road looking North from York Hill c1905.
The Hare & Hounds pub can be seen on the right with the Stanford Arms behind

London Road: A Walk on the East Side

From Preston Circus the first building on the east side is the Hare and Hounds pub. It is an imposing building constructed in the angle of the furlong. A date, 1905, above the main frontage indicates its erection but there had been a tavern there since 1795 when the main London Road was re-routed. The pub is the oldest commercial site in the road. Planning records show that permission was granted for major alterations to the building in 1902, possibly delayed until 1905 to link in with the disruption caused by the laying of the Preston Circus tramlines.

A curving building line carries the next block round into Rose Hill Terrace, from a charity shop, which was a small cobblers, to the large frontage of a Mobile Phone shop (closed in 2009) and is now Light Settings. This large site had been Mitchell's; long remembered as a specialist paint shop but one that had developed from Mitchell's original builders firm.

Below Rose Hill Terrace there is a line of small 19th century buildings. No. 78 was for many years part of the local bakery chain of Ogden's. The next few buildings reflect the rapid turnover in High Street traders; No. 79 was a milliners in 1926, a second-hand bookshop in 1951, a bakers in 1958 and since 1970 at least until recently, had been Patricia's Florists. Some enterprises have disappeared completely from the road. No. 80 was the receiving office for the Portslade based Petersfield Laundry, something that would have been seen in most commercial streets in the past, now a clothing repair shop.

High streets often contain clusters of similar premises and the northern end of London Road has drawn in a collection of technical shops on the east and the west. In this block there was a Jessop Photoshop and a computer/camera shop a few doors down. South of No. 84 there has been a great deal of change to the built structures with a distinctly different frontage, now Blockbusters, which was refronted in 1959 with the City Gate community rooms above, formerly the Co-op Hall. In complete contrast is No. 87, which is a fine Georgian house, variously in the past St. Bartholomew's and St. Peter's Vicarage, incredibly threatened with demolition in 1970 and now converted into small flats. Still in an ecclesiastical zone the 1894 New Primitive Methodist Church at No. 88 is currently empty, awaiting change of use.

The large frontage of John's Camping has replaced the 1920s occupancy of Reeves confectionery. The sequence of occupancy is interesting here, as in the post-war era Southern Junior Aircraft, Sports and Model Goods evolved into A.A. Baker's a long standing sportswear store in the 1950s, itself eventually becoming the Camping Shop and Action Bikes. The Brighton Labour Club at No. 93 had been granted building permission for conversion to a picture theatre in 1912, although there is no evidence this was ever carried out. The largest single London Road premises is the 1931 Co-op building.

Baker Street marks the field boundary separating The Crook from North Butts; this latter furlong was the first area to be developed along the London Road from 1815. Baker Street has become a busy secondary shopping street, a newsagents was on the south corner in 1926 with Mason and Mills vegetable depot next door. By the post war era a small grocery shop –Burnards– had opened, later evolving through Victor Value into Tesco, before changing use to the Nationwide Building Society in 1979. Next door at No. 106 the Timpson shoe shop was there from at least 1926 and was still recorded by the final Kelly's directory in 1974.

H. Ogden, bakers at 78 London Road on the corner of Rose Hill Terrace (1930-1962)

The last day of trading for the Premier Seed Co. at 117 London Road (1916-1963).
Next door at 116 London Road, Elliott's tool merchants suffered the same fate in the 1990s after 60 years of trading.
The Mechanic's Arms was demolished in the early 1970s and became part of Boots the Chemist.

On the corner of Marshall's Row is a good example of continuity with Principal Meats in 2006 carrying on a long tradition from at least 1926 when it was Reeves' Pork Butchers. The low building is speculated to be the oldest surviving structure in London Road. Marshall's Row leads into the Open Market and on this corner behind the butchers was located one of the great delights of London Road past, Dawkin's Forge. Directories list Mr. Dawkins as having an address of 110 London Road, but his blacksmiths was round the corner. A link with London Road's past of horse-drawn transport, Mr. Dawkins was still shoeing horses in the early sixties. The forge was up for sale in 1968 but demolished soon after. Embedded in the flint wall at the rear was a large iron tethering ring still in place until the 1980s. South of Marshall's Row is a soul-less modern block of electrical goods and a bookmakers. At one time in the early 20th century it had contained a small Co-op outfitters and Davis' seedman stores, an established business going back into the 19th century with the Elephant and Castle pub on the corner.

Francis Street, originally full of small working class dwellings, was cleared in the early sixties and is now a shadow of its former self, but the little stretch of buildings leading down to Oxford Street has an interesting clue to its former appearance. This block stuck into the road, out of line with the other buildings to north and south, and with the introduction of the trams in 1905 it was necessary to realign it. This was accomplished in 1904, as a plaque high above HSBC Bank notes. The shop next to the bank, now a newsagents, was a stationer in 1926 but in the forties and fifties was Elliott's, an upmarket tool shop. I remember it fondly because it also doubled as an outlet for Dinky Toys, with an impressive window display to delight small boys out on shopping expeditions with their mums. The corner of Oxford Street has had a diverse history of traders as various as Marley Tiles and a baker's shop/café. Early in the 20th century it was the Premier Seed Company, 'seed and bulb merchants and horticultural sundriesmen', a reminder of the agricultural past of the North Butts Furlong.

Across Oxford Street major changes to the built environment have taken place with two of the biggest of the High Street traders, Boots the Chemist and Somerfield's supermarket, occupying the block from 118-131, topped with Riley's snooker club. Eventually converted to a Fine Fare store it had been an old Brighton firm founded by Sidney Bellman. Bellman's was an innovative concern and in 1936 advertised Jersey potatoes for sale, brought by an aeroplane from the Channel Islands. Prior to Fine Fare (whose ghost of a sign can just be discerned in the brickwork above) there has been a clutch of small businesses along this stretch, two fishmongers, a confectioner, a baker next door, an ironmonger, printers, hardware store, pork butcher, piano and music shop, a tobacconist and two pubs.

Another small block lies between Oxford Place and Brunswick Row. The corner property, since 1948, the Co-op Funeral Parlour, was for many years Rice motor engineers. Its architectural style is very distinctive and similar in its 1894 detail to other Brighton buildings in Ditchling Road and North Road. Next door, Tidy the upholsterer in the 1920s gave way to a branch of Buxton's the house furnisher, now Bright House.

No. 135 listed as Nusons, 'Ham and Beef Merchants' in the twenties, had changed to Townsend's cooked meat dealers staying there until the late fifties. By 1958 this had given way to Gibbs the jewellers and is now subsumed in Bright House.

South of Brunswick Row in London Road was Gardner the grocer, incongruously becoming Betty's ladies hair stylist and later Dunn's, now Johnson's dry cleaners. A degree

Brighton & District Labour Club & Institute at 93 London Road from c1919-1965
The site became part of the Co-op extension

Advert from the Brighton & Hove Herald Coronation Supplement May 1937

of interrupted continuity can be discerned at No. 138, formerly Austen's Pie and Cake shop but now MacDonald's hamburger restaurant! For 52 years this building, decorated with a Corbin's monogram and construction date of 1933 was a local supplier of decorating materials; so distinctive was the monogram that MacDonald's were refused permission to obscure it with the 'Golden Arches' of the firm.

The Prince of Wales pub was on the corner of Queen's Place until about WW2 when it was converted to estate agents and later a building society. The large building on the south of Queen's Place, turning into St. Peter's Place was Barclays bank from early in the 20th century, possibly from 1912 when alterations took place. Rather ironically for a bank it is now used by Brighton Housing Trust whose remit is 'solutions to homelessness.'

My great grandfather, William Humphyrs, was born in Gibraltar in 1843, as his father was a Corporal serving with the 77th East Middlesex Regiment of Infantry. I don't know when he opened the shop but in the 1881 census William is listed as a watchmaker/jeweller living in a shop at 121 London Road with his wife and four sons. His son David joined the business known as W. Humphyrs & Son and in the 1901 census David is living alone at that address. He married Agatha Bridger in 1903 and had a daughter, Gladys in 1904. Gladys was my mother and her parents ran the business until David died in 1926. I can remember a black marble clock with the Humphyrs name on it but I have no idea where it is now. I have an interesting letter written by David's brother William from Harrison Camp, South Africa in 1901. It was during the Boar War and William was asking for items to be sent to him, so that he could make brooches out of coins for the troops. After my grandfather's death my grandmother and mother bought a sweet shop in Upper Gloucester Road and the shop in London Road became Silverthorne's the fishmongers and later became part of the supermarket.

Sheila Parsley

In the 1960s there was a shop called Bellman's on the corner of Oxford Street. It stocked various items, ranging from toys, watches, records, knitting patterns and wool. This later became a food store called Fine Fare where I had a Saturday job in the late 70s. On the present site of Aldi's, on the corner of Cheapside, stood the original Woolworth's. I can remember the wooden floors and shelf units.

Janice Tilley

HUMPHRYS & SON,
WATCHMAKERS & JEWELLERS,
SILVERSMITHS & OPTICIANS,
121, LONDON ROAD, BRIGHTON.

The demolition of Oxford Court in October 1938 attracted a large crowd. Oxford Street Chapel can be seen in the background next to Nos. 12 & 13 Oxford Street, later to become Pip Pirolli's ice cream shop

Corbin's, decorators & merchants at 139 London Road opened in 1874.
It is now the site of MacDonald's

Brunswick Street to Queen's Place

Queen's Place, once known as Brunswick Street, is a small mews tucked between London and Ditchling Roads. All that remains of this once thriving little thoroughfare are six flint properties and a warehouse (Nos. 3-9) which were built c1800. The Duke of Dorset originally owned this plot of land, the cottages built probably to house his workers and tradesmen. Around 1820 Prospect Place, a group of large Georgian properties was built overshadowing the cottages.

The 1822 street directory lists 16 tenements in Queen's Place and the survey map of 1826 shows two rows of cottages parallel to each other, and five cottages in Brunswick Row. The Rate Book for 1826 records seventeen tenements, most with the rateable value of one shilling and ten pence. Each comprised two rooms upstairs and two downstairs and a small rear yard. At times there were as many as eight or more people, not necessarily related, residing in any one household. Trades included blacksmiths, bricklayers, carpenters, labourers and inn waiters. In later years with the arrival of the railway, occupations altered to station porters, guards, stokers, cab drivers, grooms and gardeners

By 1841, there were ten cottages and an alehouse in Queen's Place occupied by eleven families containing twenty eight adults and thirty children. Brunswick Row's five cottages had become home to twelve adults and eighteen children.

There were many long term residents, for instance Edward Howell, house agent (1874-1884), who had No. 3, a builder's yard from 1892-1934. The existing warehouse at No. 3, its frontage altered to match the others, listed as a yard from 1892-1952. The original house had earlier been changed into a commercial business, with builders as tenants. Around 1953 No. 3 was sold and Triad Motors established.

Some residents spanned generations; as the census records indicate. No. 4's tenant was Theodore Gearing (Joiner), wife and six children from 1879-1946 (67yrs). No. 6's tenant was James Stoner (Milkman/Railway worker), wife and five children from 1881-1966 (85yrs). No. 9, the corner property was documented as the Labour Institute between 1916-1934. Nos.1 and 2 which stood at the Brunswick Row end, were demolished in the late fifties. A little later the entire row on the western side (Nos. 13-17) was demolished to become part of Corbin's warehouse. This area now contains the rear premises of a Macdonald's fast food outlet and an office & stationery warehouse.

Queen's Place east side c1950

Cyril Burgoyne, age 12 outside No. 14 Queen's Place in the summer of 1927
No. 14 was demolished to make way for Corbin's extension

No. 1 Brunswick Court in 1953 was approached by a narrow passage at the side of 25 Oxford Street
There were originally eight cottages in this small court
The site is now part of a car park behind Somerfield's supermarket

Brunswick Row

Brunswick Row grew from five tenements recorded in 1826, eleven in 1850 to fifteen by 1860.

By the 1860s the residents ranged from a cordwainer (shoemaker) to a cab maker, labourers, servants and dressmakers. Most of the properties had lodgers or nurse children (children cared for by the family). Several tenants had lived in the area for at least ten years. Three early tenants recorded were a Chelsea Pensioner, a painter and an upholsterer.

Some residents of the cottages spent many years in the area. Elizabeth Brooker ran a shop at No. 1 Queen's Place for twenty one years and then moved to No.11 Brunswick Row. She is shown as being on Parish Relief on the 1851 census after her husband's death in 1848. In 1861 she still occupies No.1 but now listed as a mangler by trade, aged then 61 and having one daughter and grandchildren in the household. She had been in the locality for over forty years and died in 1863.

By the 1860s the residents ranged from a cordwainer to a cab maker, labourers, servants and dressmakers. Most of the properties had lodgers or nurse children. Several tenants had lived in the area for ten years or more.

In 1877 a drinks manufacturer was established at No. 8 on the north side with Mathew Ellis, originally from Yorkshire, listed as the proprietor. On the 1881 census Mathew (age 49) and wife Harriet (50) are listed at No.1. He employed four men and two boys in the production of ginger beer. Water in those days was considered undrinkable, so a form of light beer was produced as the alternative, consumed by both adults and children. By the 1890s the company had expanded and started to produce mineral water with a further outlet in Oxford Place.

The small cottages were gradually considered to be unsuitable for habitation in their original state, and by 1939 only eleven were occupied and by 1954 only four still had tenants. Only a house previously owned by T. Motors, and one other remain, both now refurbished. Domestic garages owned by the council and rented out, replaced the original houses but these were eventually sold and the area cleared for redevelopment. Seven new properties were built in 2005; the exteriors styled to blend in with those in Queen's Place with flint frontages, unlike the original cottages.

Pikes Directory 1905

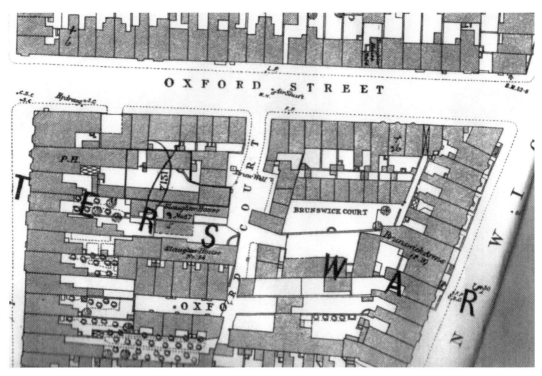

Ordnance Survey map of 1876

Ditchling Road c1905 looking north. Richardson's drapers & toy repository are on the left
(later part of Buxton's furniture stores) near to the Brunswick Arms (now Caroline of Brunswick)

Ditchling Road

First recorded as Adelphi Terrace, there were fourteen properties listed in 1822. Residents at this time included a laundress, fruitier, coal merchant, builder, glass cutter, a lodging house keeper and Mrs Blackburn's School for Ladies at No. 12. By 1833 residents included a baker, tea dealer, a solicitor, a shop and Dr. Williams at No. 5. Adelphi Terrace was renamed Brunswick Place North c1840; it then lists 43 properties in the street directory.

By 1850 street directories record up to forty-four residents with several lodging houses and a variety of trades. Joseph Sedgwick, who lived at No.5, was the Minister of the Ebenezer Baptist Chapel in Richmond Street where he is recorded as having taken services since 1833.

Family businesses survived well and records show; Mrs Simpson milliner at No. 2 from 1845-1870 (also a lodging house for 25yrs), William Sharp furniture broker at No. 12 from 1856-1878 (22yrs). Issac Hollingdale's grocers shop at No. 16, known as the Level Arms it also sold beer and traded from 1850 into the 1890s (40 yrs). George Rose, tailor at No. 19 from 1836-1861 (25yrs), Mr T. Branstone kept a lodging house at No. 26 between 1861-1892 (31yrs), Mrs E. Tyson confectioners at No.30 from 1867-1884 (17yrs) and Peter Emery had a shop at No. 36 between 1867-1891 (24yrs).

> In 1851, my great-great grandfather, Isaac Alfred Hollingdale came to Brighton from Poynings and became a beer retailer and grocer at the 'Level Arms', 16 Brunswick Place North. Isaac died in 1875 of liver disease leaving two houses and money to his sons, so the move from Poynings had been beneficial to his finances if not to his liver.

> *Thelma Dove*

From 1892 well into the 1930s Corporation baths for public usage were situated at No. 93 at the junction of Viaduct Road.

In 1901 Brunswick Place North had a name change and became 1-93 Ditchling Road which included Adelphi Terrace, a parade of Georgian Houses opposite the Level. It contained a variety of small shops; two furniture dealers, a toy shop, a post office and a greengrocers. Rose the florist at No. 63 was a confectioners in the 1900s with a sideline as a bookies in the rear of the building.

The story of how Buxton's evolved, in its day a large furniture store, is best told by a family member.

> My father, Percy Buxton, although from the East End of London, met my mother in Bournemouth and married her in 1919. I don't know why they came to Brighton but my maternal grandmother came with them and they lived above a small shop at No. 31 Ditchling Road. My father borrowed £100 from the bank and went to sales and bought various small second-hand things like wash basins and commodes. My grandmother used to clean these and the first sales book shows that they were sold for six pence or one shilling. My paternal grandparents then came to Brighton and bought No. 33 Ditchling Road and opened a business selling clothes, as a credit trader where customers paid so much a week. Over time things evolved and

Buxton's furniture dealers before rebuilding

Brook's yeast shop at No. 27 Ditchling Road c1962 just before its demolition and the rebuilding of Buxtons

gradually new and old things were sold in the shop. When my grandfather died my father took over that premises as well. It was only a small shop and my grandmother lived over the top. While I was at school I used to get asked to do a certain amount of work. One of the things I used to do, with assistance of one other person, was to deliver furniture on a handcart. We used to get the cart from Mr. Dawkins, the blacksmith in the Open Market and sometimes we had to push it all the way up Elm Grove.

We expanded the business and started to sell prams. Anytime from 1936-1980 if you mentioned Buxton's people would say 'They sell prams'. Before the war prams cost about £4 and we'd give £1 worth of presents with the purchase

We took over 27a Ditchling Road which had previously been a sweet shop and we started buying individual places in Oxford Place when they became available. The last one we bought (c1962) was No. 27, Brook's yeast shop, on the corner of Ditchling Road and Oxford Place.

During the war the shop more or less closed and only sold the prams but when I returned I opened up the furniture side of the business again. The shop front was a series of shutters that had to be taken down each day and the furniture put in the forecourt. The problem I had was that you couldn't buy new furniture without coupons. My wife and I used our own coupons to buy the first pieces of furniture. My mother was the person with the most foresight and she was the one who pushed my father on. He didn't believe that he should borrow money and he wouldn't go to the bank to borrow to extend the business. My father used to love going on holiday, so I had to do things when he was away. The Borough Surveyor used to say 'Why do I always get a planning application when your father is away?'

When we had the first extension we had a walkway made to the shop at the back. We then went into contract flooring because we didn't need a shop for that. We remained the only family-owned furniture shop in Brighton, as all the others e.g. Johnsons & Cobbs had closed. We've had three generations of the family in the business, my two sons and a grandson. We used to have a very loyal clientele and if we gave good service they would tell their children. The houses in Upper Lewes Road for instance, I think we've probably furnished some houses twice over. This sort of thing has now gone. You can give all the service you like but if people think they can get it cheaper elsewhere they won't return but if there is a mistake made there was always a Mr. Buxton to see.

Norman Buxton

Opposite: Chichester Home, 9 St. Peter's Place c1907. Originally a substantial private house, in the early 1900s it was the Y.W.C.A. Boarding House for Young Women

Prospect Place to St Peter's Place

Originally called Prospect Place, this listed terrace, with its ionic pilasters, bow fronts and balconies was possibly designed by A & AH Wilds. The building of St. Peter's Church in 1824 removed the once beautiful prospect and the name was changed to St. Peter's Place.

> Eligible Dwelling Houses in St Peter's Place near the new church to be sold by auction by Mr Creasy at the Old Ship Tavern. On Friday 11th Aug 1826 at 12 o clock. Three substantial and well built carcasses most delightfully situated and being No 1, 2 & 3 St Peter's Place one of which No 3 is nearly finished and No 2 is in a very forward state. The whole being laid down & planned for the reception of respectable families & will contain large parlours drawing rooms numerous bedrooms and all necessary offices. The great improvements which have been made at this part of Brighton & the certainty of the pleasure grounds adjacent always remaining open for the public render a residence in this neighbourhood highly desirable. Held on a lease for a term of 99 years at a ground rent with a purchasing clause. Particulars & conditions of sale may be had by Messrs Osbourne & Harrison Solicitor 13 Castle Square at the bar of the Old Ship & Mr Creasy Auctioneer North St Brighton.

> *The Brighton Herald - 5th August 1826*

Respectable families did indeed take up residence. In 1833 a Mr. R. Lawrence was registered as the treasurer for the Charitable Institute Society for Relieving the Poor Widows, another occupier was the Rev. J. Trego (Independent Minister for the Countess of Huntington Chapel c1845-1864). Residents are shown to be people living mostly on their own means, and some were listed in the court directory. Census records of 1851 prove there were several long-standing residents of a considerable age. They all employed housekeepers, cooks and servants.

James Terry, the Chief Constable of Brighton, resided in No. 8 between 1886 and 1895. Mr. Terry joined the police force in 1843 and served for 50 years. He was so well thought of, that upon his retirement, local people made a subscription of £600 to purchase Hoathly Villa at Preston for him. From c1898 to 1917 No. 8 was The Young Women's Christian Association, overseen by a Miss Battcock. In 1900 at least three of the properties were not used as private residences. Until 1917 Number 9 was listed as the Servants Registry and up to 1935 No. 7 was the Brighton Refuge for Girls. In the latter part of the nineteenth century there's an influx of physicians, surgeons or dentists residing in the properties and these professions were repeated over the years at Nos.1, 2, 5, & 8. No. 1 (formerly St Peter's House) became a bank in the early 1900s, firstly London & Provincial then Barclays; it now is the base for Brighton Housing Trust.

Ordnance Survey Map 1876 St. Peter's Place showing the long front gardens

Aeroplane view of London Road & Cheapside looking south c1910

Cheapside

Cheapside now appears to be a small, insignificant turning between the Hobgoblin Public House and Aldi's in London Road. It's familiar to most people only as a road you cross if walking to or from Brighton Station. With the few remaining houses now cast in the permanent shadow by the City College, buildings in Pelham Street and building work for the City Point redevelopment at the Station end, it seems to be the Cinderella Street of the neighbourhood.

The map of Brighton 1815 shows the 'leakways' clearly. The future Cheapside lies between the North/4th Furlong and the Short/5th Furlong. It is indicated by a track on an 1830 map between Ann Street and Trafalgar Street. By 1842, on the plan of 'Brighton and its Vicinity', it bears the name 'Cheapside'.

With the Railway Depot at one end, the entire street developed with a variety of buildings on either side. The 1842 Street Directory shows it to be a veritable hive of trading activity with cow keepers, coal merchants, three grocers, two bakers, a straw bonnet maker, a boot & shoe maker, a dressmaker, a blacksmith and a Miss Mary Butcher's ladies school.

By 1873 Page's Directory shows that the street had a coal dealer, a stonemason and a tailor. On the site of Nos. 2 & 3, Pelham Street Board School opened for boys, girls and infants.

Kelly's directory of 1898 is helpful in that it lists the streets running into Cheapside from the north and south. With our backs to London Road, we would have seen Pelham, Redcross, Whitecross, Wood, Blackman and Station Streets to the south and Providence Place, St. Peter's & Belmont Streets, Belmont Place, Fleet and Queen Street to the north. This clarifies the sites of the public houses i.e. one on nearly every corner. Other businesses now include a carver & gilder, a brush maker, a sign writer and a hairdresser.

 The longevity of some of the businesses was impressive. At No. 2 there were dining rooms from 1906 until 1960; even now the Hobgoblin Pub in its approximate location still provides food.

The school, classified in 1887 as a Board School for Boys/Girls and Infants became the site of Pelham Street Senior Girls' School and later Margaret Hardy County Secondary School annexe. The buildings are now incorporated into City College.

Two merchants, who set up shop in 1906, were there for many years. An egg merchant who traded at No 5 from 1906 – 1939 and A. Smith, a wholesale grocer traded at No. 46 & 47 until 1939 and then moved to No. 43 where he continued trading until 1970.

Private individuals also remained in the area for many years. Mrs. A Marchant lived at No. 6 and the Fanstone family at No 9 from 1927-1970. Kelly's Directory of 1898 is the last year that it gives families or traders occupying the premises from Nos. 26-37. By 1949 it is being used by British Railways (Southern region) as their coal wharf, with Messrs Corrall & Co., Shelley & Son and Harris & Sons as coal merchants.

The premises at 46 & 47 were then demolished to make way for the building of a small block of six flats that still remain today. At No. 44 Grover Hook, a well respected local French polisher, was in residence from 1920-1950 and a member of his family is still in residence today. Nos. 43 & 44 are the only two remaining original houses in the street.

By 1974 few properties are recorded and the street awaited its fate. Nos. 4-13: H. Waller & Sons – sheet metal workers - occupy the premises between 14 and 17. Whitecross Street and Wood Street are not even mentioned; only the coal wharf remains and plucky numbers 43 & 44 and the flats where 45/46 & 47 once stood.

Walking up Cheapside today, we see little evidence of the thriving community it must once have been. On the left, there is the Hobgoblin Pub with its extensive garden at the rear giving a glimpse of past glory. We then pass the City College buildings, which stretch across Pelham Street and up to Whitecross Street. Still on the left hand pavement, we pass the Nationwide Auto Centre and Warehouse and Offices for sale. Crossing Blackman Street there are more buildings with large multi-storeyed premises facing us across Station Street.

On our return journey down Cheapside we get a glimpse of things to come.

Crossing the road to reach Fleet Street there is a major new development in front of us; this area is now part of City Point Development. Building still continues, but the once derelict area showed signs of revival when a new Sainsbury's store opened in March 2007. A new residential development called Kingscote Way has now been built on the ground where once small terraced houses stood but was for so long waste ground used as a car park.

Looking back at this forlorn little street, echoing at times to the sound of hundreds of students coming and going from City College, and looking at the regeneration of a once derelict site, who could imagine they were walking an ancient track or leakway between the 4th & 5th Furlongs of the old Parish of Brighthelmstone.

> The barrow boys would regularly appear on the corner of Cheapside and Ann Street selling things and shouting. One of them would always keep an eye out for the policeman and then run away. There also used to be a man with a string fiddle who played on the corner of Cheapside.

Doris Vaughan

Oxford Street

Oxford Street was one of the earliest streets developed in the area and in 1824 there were thirty four households including a tailor, a baker and two shoemakers. The 1851 census listed thirty nine households with only six heads of household born in Brighton, twenty four from Sussex villages and towns, five from Kent and one apiece from Middlesex, Pembroke, Dorset and Surrey.

The Ordnance Survey map of 1873 shows a slaughterhouse in Oxford Street and two in Oxford Court, suggesting that the area had become a less favourable place to live and work . The Court also contained workshops and small houses, and was pronounced as unfit for habitation in the 1930s and demolished. Brunswick Court, accessed by a narrow alley beside No. 25 Oxford Street, suffered the same fate

The Oxford Street Chapel, built in 1890 by Parker Anscombe in Renaissance style, has been the Church of Christ since c1918 and still remains an active church.

Oxford Street was also the site of the Open Market during WW1 until it was moved to the Level in 1921. Bellman's draper's shop opened in the 1920's at No. 17 and transferred to a larger, more diverse store in London Road in the 1930s. It remained a popular store but closed in the 1960s.

The People's Dispensary for Sick Animals of the Poor opened in the early 30's at No.16 and the PDSA shop still remains at No.12 today.

> In the 1930s there was a small ice cream shop called 'Pips' run by an Italian couple. The ice cream was sold in separate cones of strawberry, vanilla and chocolate flavours. If you were flush with money then you could buy a three time, a special cone that took all three flavours together. I still have mouth watering memories of the big brass lids being removed from the container flooding the shop with such a wonderful smell.

David Huggins

Oxford Court accessed at 33 Oxford Street. It was demolished in 1936

Oxford Street in 1936 just before the demolition of Oxford Court on the right
Mr. F. Arbuary's general shop can be seen at the entrance of the Court

Circus Elephants walking along Baker Street towards the Level c1952

We had bought some of the areas of Oxford Court and we let these out to a couple of people who had a horse and cart and sold vegetables. Unfortunately there was quite a lot of produce lying around and there were rats. The whole of Oxford Court had blue cobblestones because ponies had been kept there for many years and I used to go and visit them as a child. The people who lived in Oxford Court were some of the roughest families in the town and there were rows and knife and fist fights.

Norman Buxton

I lived at 14 Oxford Court from the age of three. It wasn't very nice there, as it was a small cul-de-sac behind London Road with an entrance in Oxford Street. Our neighbours were a mixed bunch. There was Mr. Arbuary who had a small grocer's shop at the entrance to the court and owned some of the small houses. He sold salt that he would cut with a rusty saw into penny or tuppence pieces. Mr. Slark sold greengrocery and had a horse and cart that he rode around the area. There was also a big gypsy woman who was widowed who had a horse and cart and sold logs. She always kept everything clean and tidy. Next to us was Mrs. Thorpe who had twelve children but goodness knows where they all slept!

Our house was basically two up and two down with a large attic room where we played. We had an open grate in the sitting room where we'd burn anything to keep warm, as coal was expensive. We lived next to a slaughterhouse which backed onto my bedroom. It didn't really worry me, as it was quite a novelty for us kids. The cattle would come from the station herded by dogs down Ann Street through the big gates from London Road and then taken several at a time into the cul-de-sac to stop them escaping. If there was a crowd of them you couldn't get out of the door. Unfortunately we used to get quite large sewer rats and they used to send terrier type dogs down the drains to kill them.

I missed some school because I was often ill but my mother kept me at home on occasions to look after the other children when she went off to earn a few bob. When I left school I got a job at an oil firm in Pelham Street and I had to fetch a barrow from Mr. Dawkins the smith in the Open Market and deliver the oil. When they started to clear the slums in the 1930s we were offered a house in Wiston Road, Whitehawk and we moved there.'

Ernest Whittington

Baker Street

Baker Street runs from 104 London Road to Ditchling Road. Since its development in the early 1840s it had always been a vibrant shopping community of small businesses, shops, pubs, hairdressers and cafes. The 1851 census shows a selection of occupations including drapers, carpenters, plasterers, engine drivers, a manufacturer of patent yeast, a coal merchant, publicans and bakers. Many family businesses have continued to trade in the street for many years. For nearly eighty years, James E. Davis, a seedsman's shop, occupied Nos. 1 & 2 Baker Street before the shop was bought by the Co-op for their extension in 1932. Other businesses of long standing included Mr. Cooper of hair dressing fame, Champion's Baby Carriage dealers, Coombs Pet Shop and Bardsley's fish & chip shop. The Co-op gradually purchased the small shops on the northern side of the street from London Road to London Terrace and redeveloped the site. The Co-op's closure in 2007 could have been a catastrophe; however Baker Street still seems to be thriving with alternative businesses such as a tattoo parlour and an internet café.

In 1924, Charles & Mary Champion started a business, as suppliers of prams and baby carriages that this lasted for almost eighty years. I used to do the servicing and cleaning of the prams. They would come from the manufacturers part assembled and you used to have to put them together and clean the grease off the wheels and polish them up. If they weren't immaculate, they didn't leave the shop and that's how it always was. We had a policy that we serviced prams free of charge for life. It was this kind of service that led generations of customers to keep coming back.

Peter Champion

Granddad (Claude) was always smartly dressed; he wore a trilby hat with a feather in it and smoked a pipe. On Saturday mornings he would take my sister Lesley and me out in the van to do deliveries. We would end up back at the shop just in time for lunch of fish and chips from Bardsley's. The shop always had lots of stock and there was no where to sit, only a little wooden trike which we would fight to sit on. By the 1980s independent shops such as Champion's came under increasing pressure from the multiples such as Mothercare. My sister Andria became the fourth generation of Champion's to work at the shop but in 2002 the family decided that it was time to close the door for the final time. It was a sad day, but we didn't want to sell it on. We didn't want to go past and see a stranger running it.

Susan Hill nee Champion

Benjamin Bardsley, originally a blacksmith from Burnley, came to Brighton during the depression hoping to find work. He opened his first fish and chip shop in Upper Russell Street and later encouraged his children to follow into the business. Today only the Baker Street shop is open but it continues to be a family business, now with the fourth generation of the family working there. The business attracts celebrities, as well as loyal local custom and they have the delightful tradition of presenting each child who comes into the shop with a single wrapped chip.

Roy Brown reported in the Evening Argus 20-1-2000

My great aunt, Daisy Dawes was the proprietress of The Chocolate Shop, later called The Chocolate Box, at 24 Baker Street from the 1920s to the late 60s. Her rent was £1 a week and it never changed. Before WW2 she took in lodgers but during the war she took in her sister Ellen Moy, husband Charles and their daughter in-law Olive. Following Ellen's death in 1952, a companion, Miss Gough, lived with her. Both ladies were unmarried and lived together until Miss Gough died in 1969. Daisy died in 1974.

Paul Moy

Allan & Joan Coombs opened their shop at 19 Baker Street in November 1934.

The shop sold eggs, chickens and bird feed at first but it progressed to sell food and accessories for most types of pet. Rationing continued after the war and people would line up along Baker Street for hours before the egg lorry was due to deliver. In 1959 the family bought the house next door and operated two businesses side by side. Allan and Joan ran the pet shop and their daughter Rosemary sold gardening equipment. I joined the business in 1963 and it was my idea to turn the two shops into one. We introduced self-service for customers and turned it into a pet supermarket. Robert Harper joined us at Coombs as a part time worker when he was a schoolboy. He enjoyed working there so much that he stayed and became the manager. The shop has continued to be successful because people know the shop staff personally and have continued to receive knowable advice about their pets.

Peter Coombs interviewed by The Argus 5-11-2004

James E Davis seed & bulb merchants at 1 & 2 Baker Street, traded from the 1870s until c1930
The shop then became part of the Co-operative stores

A. Coombs, 19 Baker Street c1955
The shop opened in 1934, extended in 1959 and is still trading as Coombs Petfood Shop

Rose Hill Terrace looking east from London Road c1910

Rose Hill Terrace

Rose Hill Terrace, probably named after the nearby area of Rose Hill (now the Sylvan Hall Estate), is first mentioned in the 1851 census with nine houses and North Cottage. These more substantial houses would attract more refined residents to the area. A large proportion of these were women who were listed as fund holders (having a private income) and proprietors of houses.

By 1861 there were 71 houses with more eclectic residents including fund holders, clergymen, retired businessmen and working tradesmen. By the 1870s No. 2 had become Miss Churchyard's ladies school and there were two public houses, the London Arms at No. 31 (closed 1950s) and the Rose Hill Tavern at No. 71. Later census returns show residents such as tailors and dressmakers, retired businessmen, members of the clergy, an undertaker, doctors and dentists, tradesmen, school teachers, a brewer and railway workers occupying the houses.

Kingsbury Road and Street (previously Chichester Street) and London Terrace link the Terrace to Baker Street. Some houses in London Terrace were bought and demolished by the Co-op for extensions to their store.

In 1942 an air raid badly damaged 64-67 Rose Hill Terrace and the site was redeveloped in 1985 as Rose Hill Court. Rose Hill Mews, accessed from Rose Hill Terrace at No. 83, was built in the 1990s on the garden of St. Bartholomew's vicarage in London Road.

Today Nos. 2-8 Rose Hill Terrace still retain their long front gardens although two are now used for car parking. No. 8 retains its original balcony and front door. The four- storey houses (Nos. 9-15) still have their original railings but replacement doors and windows have altered their symmetry. No. 16 is a more substantial two-storied house with a side entrance, now a garage. This property was used by Short & Son printers for many years.

Today a dentist practice remains at No. 4 and the Rose Hill Tavern still remains a popular venue. Many of the family homes have been converted to flats and a small alteration and repair shop now trades near London Road.

The terrace has altered over the last 160 years but Rose Hill Terrace still maintains an air of faded gentility amongst the other streets surrounding London Road.

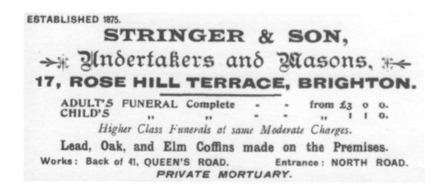

The Viaduct Road Traction Engine accident on 30th January 1908

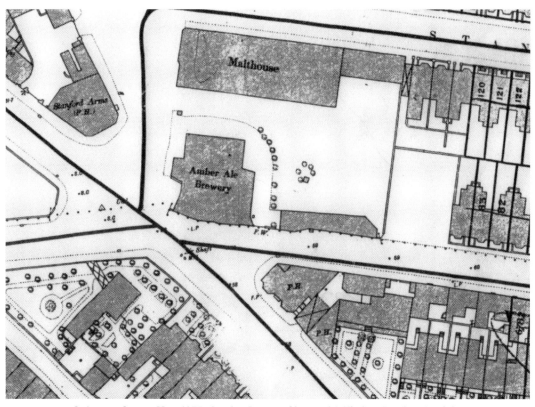

Ordnance Survey Map 1877 showing Preston Circus with Viaduct Road to the right.
The Malthouse is now the Duke of York's Cinema and the Amber Brewery is now the site of the Fire Station

Viaduct Road

Originally called Montpellier Road East, Viaduct Road marked the northern boundary of Brighton Parish and the southern boundary of Preston Parish. Of special interest were numbers 10-32, a small terrace with Ionic pilasters, dating from 1860s and formerly called Viaduct Terrace. Today the southern side of Viaduct Road shows little of its former glory. The newsagents, general shop and hairdressers have long been closed and only number six, once dining rooms, remains in commercial use as a Chinese Takeaway. The former Viaduct Terrace has lost many of its balconies and railings and many of the windows have been changed. At the top of the street the newly built Viaduct Terrace has replaced commercial buildings once containing the Gospel Mission Hall, a wireless engineer and a cane shop.

On the northern side stands the former Windsor Terrace. The yellow-brick Calvary Church was built in 1876 by James Barnes as a Primitive Methodist Church. In 1895 it then became the Railway Mission and had classrooms at the rear in Stanley Road. It is now the Calvary Evangelical Church. At the eastern end of the road stands the Brighton Business Centre. Built in 1854 as the Diocesan Training College for Schoolmistresses, it was requisitioned in 1939 by the government for use as the Royal Engineers Record Office. In 1987 it became the Brighton Business Centre.

I grew up at 2 Viaduct Road opposite the Railway Mission Church and bookshop. I used to love watching the weddings at the Railway Mission from my bedroom. My mother lived in Viaduct Road for 90 years, 60 years at No. 2 and before she married at No. 64 with my grandparents. In the 40s & 50s we could play out in the street as it was a fairly quiet road. The only day it was really manic was on race days because you'd get coaches and double decker buses with loads of people. When my mother was a child she could string a rope across the road and play skips. Obviously there wasn't much traffic then, as it was mainly horse and carts.

My gran never had an inside toilet or bathroom and she had five children in this three bedroomed house. After my parents moved in across the road she would always come over to our house for a bath. When you went into gran's house there was a passage with a front room off it but we never went in there. The kitchen was at the back and that's where they all sat round a little wooden table that gran scrubbed and scrubbed until it was white. Then there was a scullery with the old domed copper in the corner. We spent as much time at our gran's house as we did at our own. We'd just run across the road which was so quiet. The door was always left open even when she went out and it wasn't until the 60s that the family started locking doors. My gran had a front garden with a lawn and flowers. All the houses on the north side had little gardens and weren't concreted over as they are now. Out the back my grandfather grew runner beans and other vegetables, as well as flowers. He was a great lover of lupins and dahlias and he surrounded the outside toilet with golden rod in order to hide it.

Viaduct Road was very different then with a variety of shops. Mr. Selby the bootmaker lived and worked at No. 3 until it was sold in the 1960s. It then became many different shops and was finally converted into flats for students. No. 7 was a double fronted shop with two rounded windows and a door in the centre. We used to call it the Cook Shop but it was really a café that provided good old fashioned workmen's meals; now it's the Chinese takeaway. No. 8 was Mr. Budd the printer who was still there last time I visited the area. No. 9 was a little grocery store, called Willmer's. The shop was just a door and a small window with a sloping shelf displaying a few items. Inside there was an old wooden counter with a few glass cabinets and shelves at the back with packets of Cornflakes on them. They sold sweets, tins of food, washing powder, crisps and cigarettes. I can remember Mr. Willmer sitting in the corner of the shop with his trilby hat on, smoking away. My gran used to like a bit of a flutter and Willmer's was where she went to place her bets. Brenda Willmer used to open really early in the morning, as her main trade was selling tobacco and cigarettes to men on their way to work – hence the betting sideline because there weren't betting shops in those days. There had never been any electricity in the house and there were still gas mantles, so there was no washing machine, television, fridge or any indoor services. Brenda was still open in the 1960s when trade wasn't very good. The stock was often out of date but mum still bought the occasional item from her because Brenda had been my mother's friend all her life. Brenda never married, as her sweetheart had been killed in the war and she never changed her hairstyle after that. When my mother lost her sight Brenda used to take her to the bus stop and put her on the bus, so that she could come to see me.

In the 70s the road began to get busier and by the 80s it was horrendous. My mum would sit in her lounge and if a lorry or bus stopped outside her house waiting for the traffic lights to change the windows would rattle. Mum would get a piece of paper and stuff it down between the sash windows to stop the noise. In fact when the road changed to a one-way race track it was better for her because she no longer had all the traffic waiting outside her house and you would get lulls when the lights changed. It's a very different road now from when my mum used to talk to passers by, as she swept the pavement in front of her house.

Sylvia Everett

York Hill

The development of York Road North started in the 1840s, the name changing to York Hill in the early 1900s, possibly to save confusion with York Road in Hove. By 1875 there were twelve shops, three public houses and a beer house. Next to the 'Fitter's Arms Inn' at No.27, a Lecture Theatre was opened financed by Henry Willett, a wealthy businessman. This was in connection with the Brighton City Mission established in the area in 1849. The aim of the Mission was visit the sick and dying, reading the scriptures and urging than to attend public worship and to send their children to Sunday school. Open air meetings were held at the Level especially in the summer. They also visited many pubs and beer houses.

York Hill suffered with the redevelopment of the area, firstly in the early 1900s and then again in the 1960s. The street is now a short cut though from London Road between the Branch Tavern and Richer Sounds with little sign of the vibrant community it once contained.

> My family moved to York Hill in 1950. At the time it was the last house at the top of the hill, almost on the corner of New England Street. The houses were terraced with no front gardens with grills in the pavement to give light to the basement window. Many people used their front room for special occasions, but we did everything in ours, as our back room was used as another bedroom for my aunt. There were also two bedrooms upstairs. There was a small kitchen and a toilet in the garden but no bathroom. There was a tin bath that was kept in the basement and I would have a bath in front of the oven with the oven door open, so that I was kept warm. We didn't have running hot water only cold, so the water had to be heated.

> York Hill was quite steep, so the pavements had ridges crossing it. This gave us better grip especially if it was icy and we held onto the window sills when we were going up.

> The community was very stable and we had very good neighbours. At No. 13 there was a lady who'd travelled the world as a journalist … as she got older she got quite cantankerous but my mother still went round and gave her the odd meal. Next door was Croydon's the newsagent and further down the hill on the corner of London Street, there was a greengrocer's run by Mrs Ansell, a big buxom lady with massive gold rings on every finger, she was lovely.

> Opposite us there was a Mission Hall and every Sunday morning there was a Salvation Army band playing virtually outside my door. At the end of the day there would be hordes of railway men from Brighton station who would pass my house. They all wore cloth caps and a few of them would give me sweets.

> When I was a teenager, it became apparent that we would eventually move, especially when New England House was built. We were under the hammer for a long time and then in 1968/9 we were offered a flat in Thornsdale at the bottom of Albion Hill. It was lovely to have a bathroom, running hot water and an indoor toilet.

Margaret Stewart

Providence Place in 1964 just before the start of demolition

Household, Stable, and Saddlery Brushes.

BRIGHTON BRUSH WORKS,

𝔚holesale 𝔅rush 𝔐anufacturers

(Established 1873).

GOOD QUALITY, WORKMANSHIP AND FINISH.

Particular Attention given to Orders for SPECIAL PATTERNS.

GOVERNMENT CONTRACTORS.

Office and Manufactory—

53, PROVIDENCE PLACE, BRIGHTON.

Advertisement from Pike's Directory 1905

Providence Place

Providence Place was developed from 1842-47. This narrow road running behind the west side of London Road was once known as an area containing small businesses and workshops.

Providence Place was once lined with shops, houses and business premises including a forge. It was dustbin day and the streets had a meaner look than usual. Tin bins overflowed outside some of the front doors in the street whose brave sounding name belied the reality. Together with London, New York, Fleet Streets and Belmont Place they nestle in a cramped, crowded triangle stretching down from Brighton station to London Road.

Built more than 100 years ago mainly for the railwaymen, they show all show signs of being worn out, weary. Even now the dead hand of the planners can be seen everywhere. Desolate, boarded up fronts; sightless windows.

Last night Brighton's council granted clearance orders against 129 of them. …It is the first step in Brighton's latest major slum clearance project.

Evening Argus 27th January 1967

My father's family lived at 1 Providence Place, which was parallel to London Road. Samuel Prior, my grandfather was said to been a confectioner but he was also listed in the 1891 census as a 'Fly Proprietor' (owner of a small horse drawn carriage). I know that he drove a horse drawn cab from a rank at St. Peter's Church and probably stabled the horse in Providence Place, as the area had many stables and workshops at that time. By the 1901 census the family had moved to 42 London Street and my grandfather was listed as 'Living on his own Means.'

Mrs G. Payne

I attended St. Bartholomew's school in Providence Place, which in those days was at the end of the church just round the corner from Ransom's, the shop that seemed to sell everything. Opposite Ransom's there was a small music shop with a red fascia. I can still remember the violins in the window. Providence Place was used as our school playground. One of the teachers would stand at the end with a whistle and if a car was coming round the corner he would blow the whistle three times and we'd all get on the pavement.

Gordon Dean

Opposite: The picture shows Nos. 13, 14 & 15 London Road in c1903 just before the front gardens were removed for road widening

The Lost Gardens of London Road

The Street Gardens of Brighton … are in general very neatly kept, more especially on the London Road, on both sides of St. Peter's Church.

(The Gardener's Magazine 1842)

Around this time Brighton was probably the most fashionable resort in the country. The new railway line was bringing hordes of summer trippers and the autumn season was the preserve of the upper classes. From October to December the fine houses and hotels along the seafront were occupied by aristocrats and the very rich, seeking to escape the fogs of London. Here the wealth was conspicuous, the nobility and gentry, dressed in the latest fashions, paraded along the seafront and engaged in a busy round of social pursuits.

Just a few streets away, the slums were on a par with anything that might be seen in the northern industrial cities, causing a local doctor, William Kebbel, to state, 'In no town throughout the kingdom do cleanliness and filth meet in such extremes as this'.

London Road, however, was populated largely by the middle classes. In 1841 the New Monthly Magazine noted that the houses there were ' … of small but neat box-like description, … probably inhabited by retired tradesmen, the widowed families of deceased clergymen, and such that have seen better days, and who retire to spots where poverty is not wholly divested of comfort, and a humble exterior is still accompanied by respectability.'

London Road Chapel procession along London Road c1900.
The houses in the background have already started their conversion to shops

Their gardens had come under scrutiny in The Gardener's Magazine, a popular periodical which had for some years been enthusing and educating the middle classes. John and Jane Loudon who produced it were, by then, the celebrity gardeners of the day. They toured Britain, visiting towns and villages, and writing about everything they saw in great detail.

John Claudius Loudon (1783-1843) was a polymath. The most influential horticultural journalist of the time, he had also designed several large gardens which, like the Derby Arboretum, England's first public park, and Birmingham Botanical Gardens remain as a tribute to his vision. Jane Webb Loudon (1807-1858) met her husband after he had reviewed her first novel in the Gardener's Magazine. As well as collaborating with him she produced many books of her own, rivalling her husband's prodigious literary output.

They visited Brighton together on several occasions and wrote about it in the magazine. Residents of Bayswater, they compared Brighton with where they lived.

> There is a degree of neatness, select planting and high keeping, which is far from being common, in the same proportion, in the street gardens of London. Not only were grand gardens of interest but the Loudons attached considerable value to the 'common front garden.'

> It is of great importance to the advancement of gardening that the art should be displayed to as great a perfection as possible in those gardens which are most universal, which are continually under the eye of a large city population; seen by the whole country's inhabitants when they visit towns and which chiefly come under the eye of foreigners.

Though after their first visit in September 1838, they wrote:

> We are particularly gratified by the high style of planting … exhibited in some of the front gardens of some of the houses facing the London Road. Not only did they contain many of the finest hardy and half-hardy annuals, but pelargoniums, fuchsias, calceolarias, lobelias, salvias and other greenhouse plants, scarcely anything can surpass the neat manner in which many of these were tied up; and all appeared remarkably healthy and free from insects.

Not only did they see a fine range of plants in good condition but they were impressed by the ingenious ways they were displayed:

> In some of the gardens were stages of plants in pots; and we observed, in one or two, frameworks of green-painted wire of different forms for containing plants; but, instead of these frames, or cases, being filled with pots in the ordinary manner, they were lined with turf, the green side outermost, and the grass kept closely clipped, as it protruded beyond the wire.

They singled out several gardens near St. Peter's church for detailed descriptions:

> York Place – No. 14. The centre bed was surrounded by turf, with a marginal border; and the soil, both of the central bed and the border, was raised at the rate of about 4in. in a foot, so that the central bed formed an oblong cone, perhaps 8ft. by 5ft. at the base, and 2ft. high.

This was in their opinion the best front garden they saw in Brighton; it amply demonstrated the current fashion for bedding plants, to give a very bright display of colour.

> In the central bed were Salvia coccinea, (red) and Physostegia imbricata (mauve obedient plant), most splendidly in flower; Verbena chamaedrifolia (red); Fuchsia longiflora and microphylla (red); 6 or 8 varieties of heartsease, pelargoniums (red) and various other plants. In the surrounding border were Eccremocarpus scaber (orange Chilean glory vine), Potentilla atrosanguinea (red cinquefoil), chrysanthemums and 10 or 12 distinct varieties of heartsease. (Plate 1)

To a modern-day gardener heartsease is a little wild pansy, which would be insignificant in such a display, but the description goes on to note that, '… the heartseases both in the bed and border, were of the most extraordinary luxuriance and beauty; all trained to single green-painted rods and forming blunt-pointed cones, covered with flowers from the base to the summit; one or two of them nearly as high as 3ft!' Clearly he cannot be referring to tiny wild flowers!

Apart from the bedding plants, the garden also had some shrubs; 'numerous Bengal and other roses; and a most luxuriant plant of Ribes sanguineum.' This flowering currant, was a recent introduction, brought back from North America for The Horticultural Society (not yet dubbed 'Royal'), and serves to show that whoever tended that garden was, horticulturally speaking, very up to date.

Number 17's garden was almost as beautiful. 'The pyramids of heartsease were remarkably fine.' Bartonia aurea (now called Mentzelia linleyi) a bushy annual with fragrant yellow flowers, was 'trained to a rod, and petunias and Mimulus moschatus were conspicuous.' This latter, the yellow creeping musk had been brought from North America early in the century and was all the rage with Victorian gardeners. When handled it gave off a wonderful musky scent which, mysteriously, has now been lost in modern plants.

Another garden contained some wonderful climbers:

> No.19. A plant of Lonicera grata (a honeysuckle), on the side of the house, had reached the cornice, and was magnificently in flower from the ground to that height; the pendent shoots terminating in bunches of blossoms, hanging down in the most wild and graceful manner. Clematis vitalba, slightly intermixed with the larger convolvulus, had been trained by means of a few packed threads, from the side fence to the balcony on the first floor. The clematis was covered with its white fragrant blossoms, and, with the large flowers of the convolvulus, looked like a piece of flowered muslin drapery, put up to shade the parlour window.

At first reading the mention of Clematis vitalba, otherwise known as traveller's joy, and Convolvulus, bindweed, is unbelievable. Neither now is welcome in a small garden, and, as early as 1597, bindweeds had been described by Gerard as 'unprofitable weedes and hurtfull unto eche thing that groweth next unto them (sic).' However in Jane Loudon's book The Ladies' Flower-Garden of Ornamental Perennials (1844), one of the illustrations shows bindweed grouped with morning glories, so perhaps Victorian gardeners were brave enough to use them, apparently with pleasing results. (Plate 2)

Kew Plate 1

Kew Plate 2

Kew Plate 3

Kew Plate 4

York Place provided yet more material for the Loudons: 'No. 16. A very selectly planted garden, in which Lobelia gracillis, Anagallis coccinea grandiflora (pimpernel), and verbenas made a conspicuous appearance.'

Finally, in York Place, No. 21 was praised for its 'fine assortment of dwarf China asters! These are the lovely bright annual type which Gertrude Jekyll was later to describe as having 'rather harsh and discordant colours'!

In St. Peter's Place the front gardens were larger and No. 4 'contained a splendid collection of dahlias, beautifully in flower.' And also, in the surrounding border, 'roses of different kinds, Cydonia japonica (flowering quince), Mezerium, (a daphne) and other shrubs, and herbaceous plants, for display in early spring and during summer.'

On a later visit to Brighton in May 1842, it was reported that 'Brompton stocks and wallflowers were thriving (Plate 3) and the columbine 'in all its varieties' was 'in great abundance and vigour, (Plate 4) the double red lychnis, and in some places the double yellow marigold;' and red and white valerian were 'just beginning to expand their blossoms.'

The overall effect was still fashionably kaleidoscopic.

The Loudon's were informed that:

> A number of these gardens ... belong to retired London tradesmen, who look after them themselves; and scarcely any of them are under the care of jobbing gardeners.

But what of all those lovely front gardens? There are still three or four in St. Peter's Place but the ones at the west end, including No. 4, have been turned into car parks. If you walk along York Place it is difficult to imagine that there were ever any gardens, however tiny, as they are now all under the pavement. The 1876 OS map shows that the grander houses at the south end of London Road had much bigger front gardens. Didn't the Loudon's see these or were the others just so spectacular that they put them in the shade? The photo gives a glimpse of some of them in 1900. Three years later the roadway was widened for trams, after which the gardens were lost forever.

The Level

Once known as the North Steine, the Level was originally a marshy area of open land which included the present Park Crescent site and Victoria Gardens. It was always a popular venue for fairs, celebrations and demonstrations and when the North Steine was enclosed in 1817 it became the only remaining recreational area in town. Cricket was played on the Level from at least the mid 18th century, and the northern part was laid out as a cricket ground for the Prince of Wales in 1791; both the Prince and his brother the Duke of York were keen players and spectators of the game.

In the early 1800s, George Prince of Wales and later Regent watched boxing matches where betting of gold sovereigns was prevalent. Later an ox would be roasted on the Level for the benefit of the poor people of the town. The field was sometimes the setting for cruel dog fights, bear baiting & cock fighting. It was also used as a drill and exercise ground for cavalry & infantry soldiers stationed in the barracks in Church Street. In 1809 the Brighton & Hove Herald reported that 'The fair on the Level was the scene of no considerable bustle. Roundabouts, gingerbread, toy and fruit stalls were in abundance.'

The last great cricket match on the Lord of the Manor's ground took place in 1822, when Brighton beat Dorking by seven runs.

In 1822 the Level was vested by Thomas Read Kemp and other landowners in trustees on behalf of the town. They had decided that the Level was being wasted, with an open ditch dividing it, to carry off the surplus water when the Lewes Road springs rose in the winter. The entire field south of Ireland's pleasure gardens was presented to 'inhabitants and visitors … for the improvement of the town.' It then became controlled by the Brighton Commissioners, who later became the council.

It was frequently used for cricket. The matches were well supported and when a resident named Osbaldston arranged a match between Sussex and All England, with a prize of 1,000 guineas for the winning team, the Sussex players easily netted the prize money.

Little was done to improve the field until Lewis Slight, Clerk to the Town Commissioners, decided to plant a double belt of trees, with a wide pathway. The original 1,000 trees, were a gift from the Third Earl of Chichester; Thomas Pelham, who lived at Stanmer Park. They were planted in two lines on the east, north & west sides. Planting started on November 4th 1845. Lewis Slight's plans for improving the Level included the laying out of gardens under the direction of Amon Wilds the younger, and Henry Phillips, a well known local botanist and landscape gardener. Unfortunately the commissioners were reluctant to spend money on what had for years been regarded as waste land. Except for the planting of the perimeter trees and footpaths, little was done to improve Mr. Kemp's gift, and the southern area of the Level remained rough and neglected until the children's playground was built in 1927. In 1899 John George Bishop who was editor of the Brighton Herald, had called the Level 'a reproach to the town.'

The present day auctioneer's office at the south end of the Level has had various uses.

> …the (Watch) Committee had resolved, 'That a Surveyor do prepare a plan and estimate of expense of erecting a police and fire engine house for the northern part of the borough within the Level enclosure, on the west side of the southern entrance.'

Aeroplane view of Ditchling Road and the Level c1907

The police and fire engine house for north Brighton 1865-1919

Brighton & Hove Herald 18th June 1862

The branch police station (1865-1919) then became the main office for Brighton Parks and Gardens Department and was later used as a changing room for sports teams using the Level. The formal southern entrance to the Level is decorated with ornamental dolphin shaped lamps and now has a small converted café to the right. The Level has seen many changes during the years, a large skateboard park was added in the 80s and many of the fine elm trees were uprooted in the storm of 1987.

> Over 20,000 people watched a bonfire procession which marched to the Level accompanied by bands, banners, flaming torches and three effigies. The bonfire described as being as big as a small dwelling house.

Brighton & Hove Herald 1880

Over the years the Level has been used for celebrations, political and union rallies, demonstrations, sports, the annual fair and circus and impromptu gatherings of all kinds.

> When I was eight years old I attended the Oxford Street Sunday School. Returning home one Sunday we walked slap bang into a meeting with Sir Oswald Mosley's fascist 'Black Shirts' on the Level wearing their black shirts, black boots and they had shaved heads. They seemed to tower over the Brightonians who were shouting abuse at them. There were awful fights and scuffles going on.

Marie Banfield

My brother and I spent many happy days on the Level. Half of it was just rough ground to kick a ball about, but the other half had many delights for small boys. There was a boating pool divided into sections by stone bridges. I lost many small boats there slowly sinking just out of reach. Sometimes I used to run round the edge of the pool forgetting that it stopped suddenly, as it reached the bridges. Several times I ran off the edge into the water. Then it was straight home on the tram leaving a pool of water under the seat.

Guy Fawkes Day was very popular in the 1930s. The Level would look like Dante's Inferno because everyone took their rubbish to the Level, lit a fire on rough ground and let their fireworks off. We thoroughly enjoyed walking in and out of the fires, dodging the fireworks thrown by the foolish. One year a little lad had a huge banger thrown at him that unfortunately went inside his Wellington boot. His injuries were very severe and his cries of pain bloodcurdling to hear.

David Huggins

We used to play football matches on the Level – 35 a side – I kid you not – but we hardly ever saw the ball with that many playing. Two coats would go down for the goal and off you went. There was a static water tank on the Level and you had to get a pair of steps to see how much water there was. A friend of ours 'blagged' a place over Lewes Crescent and he came over and dived into the tank. We were playing football and the police came asking if he was there. When they'd gone we formed a half circle around him and ushered him into the bushes. He got away that night but they caught him in the end. During the war my mum worked at the R.E. Records office canteen that was in a Nissen hut on the Level.

Gordon Dean

We used to play on the Level where the pond used to be with the pillars, archways and bridges all around. It's a shame that they've bricked it all up. They had two big sets of swings, smaller swings and a roundabout all supervised by two Park Keepers who were always smartly dressed in their uniforms. There were loop type railings all around the edge but you could go in any time. Where the skate boarders' track is now was once all lawn and trees.

David Guildford

One of our greatest pleasures as kids in the 30s was to go down to the Level and play football. At the entrance to the Level, near the market, public meetings were held and this particular evening there were two meetings, the 'Black Shirts' (British Nazis) and the Communist Party. Invariably these meetings ended in violence between the opposite parties. It was about 9 pm, time to pack up and go home, when two men came over and asked if we would like to join a club. Thinking it was a football club we agreed and went with them to their headquarters in Oxford Place. We were given drinks, sandwiches and cakes and they took details of our names and addresses and invited us back the following evening to sign up and receive our membership cards. When I explained the reason for being so late home to my dad, he showed his temper and warned me never to go near the place again. If I remember rightly my dad said that the two men were brothers and were leaders of the local Communist Party. This was their way of recruiting young members.

Frank Edwards

My father was born in 1903 into a Lincolnshire farming family and his first job when he left Park Street school at fourteen was on the barrow for Mr. Whitehead who had a greengrocer's stall in the Open Market on the Level. I can always remember my dad taking me to the Level at Easter. We all got our skipping ropes out on Good Friday, I don't know why. He also took me there to watch the game of 'Bat and Trap'. It was a bit like rounders but you hit a lever and the ball jumped up and it was hit. Bonfire night on the Level was hell for me because I was scared stiff. There used to be hundreds of bonfires and they used to let these Chinese Crackers off and I was hopping about. The Level was all grass and it used to be ruined by the bonfires.

Beryl Tucknott

In the 50s it was exciting to watch the huge bonfire gradually appear on the Level during the weeks before November 5th. People brought every piece of old furniture, cardboard box or rubbish they could lay their hands on until you believed that it would topple over. The other annual event was the visit of the Chipperfield's or Bertram Mill's Circus who would sometimes walk their elephants along the streets.

To a young child this was a magical scene that I enjoyed more than watching the circus itself.

Years later I played for a netball team that met on the Level every Friday night. We all came straight from work and changed in the tiny, rather dank building at the south end of the Level. It was while we were changing on 22nd November 1963 that we heard the news of the assassination of John Kennedy.

Eva Le Grice

After WW 2 it took a long time for the Army to vacate some of the sites it had commandeered during the hostilities, and the Level was scarred by Nissen huts for years. Brighton Town Council decided yesterday to call in the aid of their M.Ps to release this section of the Level, the town's traditional open space, from the War Office regulation. … Ald. S. Davey said 'Unless strong action is taken these huts will be there forever.'

Brighton & Hove Gazette 26-9-1951

The Women's Peace Camp on the Level began on 15th February 1983. Its purpose was to show sympathy and support for Greenham women on trial at Newbury. It was bitterly cold and the camp lasted for two months.

Evening Argus

Today the Level is the site of annual fairs, dog walkers, skate boarders, adults and children relaxing, political and social meetings. Unfortunately it has recently suffered from adverse publicity over several incidents of abusive behaviour. Brighton & Hove Council have now started a consultation period on the future of the Level and hopefully the steady decline will cease and the area will once again revert to the earlier 'pleasure gardens' for all.

Vera Burtenshaw with her doll enjoying the Level c1930

These Nissen huts stayed on the Level for several years after WW2

Children playing at the Level c1930

Lileywhite's stall on the Level c1921. The Open Market moved from the Level to Marshall's Row in 1926

Coaches – Trams – Buses

Ask anyone the name of the main road into Brighton and they will say 'London Road'. This was not always the case, as in the early 1700s the poor condition of many of the roads made some routes into Brighton impassable in bad weather.

After 1790, and up until 1820, many of the roads into Brighton became turnpikes, the most southerly toll house on the Patcham-Preston route into Brighton being near the Crown and Anchor public house at Preston. Gradually, as drainage improved, the route into the town via Patcham was developed but via Cuckfield and Clayton

The advent of the railway to Brighton in 1841 finally brought the coaching era to an end. Brighton Corporation had been considering using trams from the late 1880s, but it was not until 1899/1900 that a bill promoting a tramway system was put forward to parliament. This bill set the framework for the system as opened on 25th November 1901, but it still did not bring tram operation to London Road.

The omission of London Road, perhaps owing to objections raised by existing horse bus operators, bemused both residents and traders alike. But in 1902 another tramway bill was passed to allow London Road to receive a track. By 1903 trams reached New England Road and Beaconsfield Road via London Road and the track in Viaduct Road ceased to be used. At the same time the main tram terminus was moved to Old Steine.

The introduction of trams had caused some changes to the urban landscape. In order to allow the trams to turn sharply from Viaduct Road into Beaconsfield Road, it had been necessary to demolish part of Longhurst's Amber Ale Brewery on the north-west corner of Viaduct Road. Mr. Longhurst lived in a large villa opposite his brewery on the corner of London Road and New England Road, where Lloyds Bank is now. The Corporation had a long battle with him, because they originally wanted the whole site of the Brewery for their tram depot, and proposed that the bottling plant (all that was left of the old brewery) be transferred to the old Gaiety Theatre in Park Crescent Place. In the event, the Government, in passing the tramway bill, restricted the corporation's compulsory purchase of the brewery site. After all the fuss, Mr. Longhurst transferred his bottling operation to the Gaiety site, the council obtained all of the old brewery but then decided that the land was too wet and marshy to take the weight of tramcars because of the Wellsbourne underground stream. Strangely part of the site was developed as a Fire Station, and was able to take the weight of several fire engines!

In 1902, following an incident between a horse bus and a tram, the owner, Walter Tilley, sold out to the corporation. The last of the horse bus operators, dating back to around 1867, disappeared from the scene.

It is thought that other buildings in London Road were demolished to allow for road widening for the trams, but there are few records to confirm this. The Hare and Hounds pub was rebuilt in 1905, but not for any obvious road widening, although the Branch Tavern and the Northern Hotel (The Hobgoblin) were also rebuilt around this time, comparison with an 1874 OS map does not indicate any road realignment and earlier Victorian buildings abut and protrude into the road. In 1905 buildings between Francis Street and Oxford Street were rebuilt and set back slightly from the original building line and these may well have been part of a road widening scheme for the trams.

As the town moved into the 1930s, it became apparent that there was a call for a more comprehensive system. The tramway needed to be extended north towards Hollingbury and Moulsecoomb during the 1920s and this had led to acrimonious council debates over costs and methods. The open-top trams were decidedly early Edwardian in appearance. In 1929, an attempt to obtain joint working between the bus company Tillings and the Corporation did not find public favour in town polls held in December.

Then there was an unfortunate incident in Ditchling Road, when a tram careered down hill past the Sylvan Hall estate, through the traffic lights at Viaduct Road, killing a cyclist and finally overturning outside the Open Market. The Corporation now seemed to accept that the tram system was inefficient. Accordingly in November 1935 they erected trolleybus overhead wires around the Level, hiring a vehicle from Portsmouth in order to undertake public trials. In December another trolleybus was hired from London Transport for a similar trial, so that the public could vote on tram to trolleybus replacement in a town poll the following January. Whilst the poll was in favour of trolleybuses, parliament threw out the bill required to undertake the changeover, as MPs regarded the situation as chaotic if the bus company was not involved. After much debate throughout 1937/38, an agreement was struck between Brighton Corporation and the bus company for a joint network for the towns. The trams would go, and both companies would provide services operated by buses and trolleybuses. The only hindrance was caused by Hove Council who, as in the past, had refused to let trolleybuses into their Borough. This agreement was to operate from April 1939 until March 1959.

After the war there was little change to the transport scene on London Road. Southdown operated routes into Sussex and the express service to London and Brighton Hove & District operated the routes to Patcham. During the period 1948-1951 the trolley bus routes extended and routes 46 and 26 travelled to the rapidly developing Hollingbury Estate.

With the 1939 agreement between the Corporation and BH&D ceasing in March 1959, both parties now wanted to include Southdown to bring about greater rationalization. They hoped to combat falling passenger traffic, so in March 1959 all trolley services ceased except those to Hollingbury and Fiveways. These continued until 30th June 1961, when Brighton Area Transport Services (BATS) was set up. All that is left of the trolleybus empire in the North Butts area are the rosettes on the Fire Station and the old Co-op building that supported the overhead wires.

Probably the most significant recent change in London Road is the creation of the Traffic Management scheme. Initially the change was relatively small, with a one way system south bound with bus lanes starting at St Peter's Place. In the 1990s, this was expanded to include a one way system right round the North Butts boundary. The main London Road A23 traffic was then diverted up Viaduct Road into Ditchling Road and via Waterloo Place into Lewes Road and Grand Parade. London Road southbound is mainly, but not exclusively restricted to buses and taxis, the intention being to improve the shopping environment. Its success is debatable, as congestion from car traffic has not been eased, especially in the summer and London Road's decline as a shopping centre has not been halted. In the southern part of London Road, congestion caused by buses queuing at the stops is as bad as before.

Back in the 1970s, there were many plans to divert the A23 around London Road, through parts of North Laine and into the New England area. One plan even envisaged a flyover at Preston Circus but this never came to fruition because of the cost and the demolition involved. With the development in the New England Quarter it looks as if London Road will remain the North South artery into the heart of the city.

The Tramway snow plough at Preston Circus travels south along London Road on 29th December 1908

Workers laying the tram lines in London Road c1903
The Hare & Hounds pub on the left was rebuilt In 1905

The Shepherd & Dog pub at 126 London Road in 1923
Originally a private house built in the early 19th century it was demolished in the 1960s

Historic Hostelries

London Road

Towards the latter part of the 19th century, if you lived in or around the London Road area and fancied a drink, you would have the choice of some 23 pubs. There were a further 25 pubs available in the area west of London Road, up to the railway and from Trafalgar Street north to Preston Circus. Today just nine establishments remain.

Building in the area had started between 1738 and 1750 and the first public house was called the Nag's Head. Located centrally in a little street that is now called Queen's Place (now solicitor's offices), it was originally an Inn and Coach House used by wagoners conveying merchandise to Brighton from London and the Sussex countryside. At this time the Nag's Head faced south and had an uninterrupted view of the area now known as Grand Parade and Victoria Gardens. A plate showing the distance from London to Brighton as 52 miles once stood just west of the Nag's Head. Later in the 1860s, it became the site of the County House Tavern (renamed The Prince of Wales in the 1870s), on the corner of London Road and Queen's Place.

The Nag's Head had no competition until around 1822, when The Elephant and Castle pub was built on the north of Francis Street and London Road (currently Forfars). This pub was also described as an Inn and Livery Stable and was close to the blacksmiths, (later Dawkin's Forge) at the end of Marshall's Row.

The Hare and Hounds, named after the Brighton Harrier Dog Kennels in that location, was built earlier in 1795 and the appropriately named Fox beer house opened next door. The remaining London Road pubs were added in the period 1830 to 1870, many being opened as beer houses

By the 1830s the Branch Tavern was in existence on the west side of London Road at Nos. 53/54. The name possibly reflects the numerous small orchards that existed in the gardens of the large houses to the north of the site. However, an alternative view is that the pub was used for early trade union activity and was named the Branch accordingly. The Elephant & Castle was also opened at this time, along with the Lamb & Flag at 124 London Road, now occupied by Somerfield's. In the 1840s, the Mechanic's Arms was opened on the corner of Oxford Street at 119 London Road (now the site of Boots the Chemists). The London Road Inn was opened next door at 120 London Road in the mid 1800s, changing its name to the Duke of Connaught in 1876.

The Great Northern Hotel was established on the corner of York Place and Cheapside in the 1860s and the final pub to open in London Road was the Grapevine (1871) at No.21 London Road.

Brunswick Place North (later Ditchling Road)

In the 1830s two pubs opened in Brunswick Street North, the Brunswick Arms (later called the Leek & Winkle and now Caroline of Brunswick) and the Druid's Arms. Both pubs are still in existence although the Druid's Arms was originally much smaller. By 1850, the North Star Tavern was added at the corner of Francis Street (now North Star Studios) and the Northern Tavern at the corner of Kingsbury Street. In the 1870s two pubs opened, the Bat and Ball (named after the game Bat & Trap played on the Level) on the corner of

Oxford Street and the Level Arms beer house and grocer's shop (later becoming part of Buxton's Furniture shop).

Side Streets

On the north side of Oxford Street there were two pubs, the Oxford Arms at 21/22 opened in the 1840s and in the 1890s the Volunteer Arms, changing to the Volunteer Artillery Man by 1900 and then reverting to its original name.

In Baker Street, the Mitre Arms was opened in 1850, whilst in Rose Hill Terrace two pubs were established in the 1860s, the Rose Hill Tavern at No. 71 and the London Arms opposite at No. 31.

In 1854 Cheapside boasted two public houses the Cross Keys Inn and the Engineer Inn plus five beer shops: the Joiner's Arms, Brighton Arms, Railway Arms, Queen's Head and the Belmont Arms.

The following press cutting gives an indication of what a pub might provide in way of amusement:

> Cross Keys Inn, Cheapside, Brighton will sell by auction (in consequence of the expiration of the lease), on Friday 11th June1856 at 11 am, a quantity of useful household furniture and a bagatelle board with balls, cues and stand.

> *Brighton Gazette, Thursday 10th June 1856*

By 1887 the Orange Tree public house had replaced the Ladies School at No.42 listed from 1842. By 1939 only three of these remained, the Cross Keys, Railway Arms and the Queen's Head and by 1974 only the Queen's Head valiantly remained.

To the west of London Road, sandwiched between Trafalgar Street, New England Road and the railway works, were numerous beer houses. Many of the names reflected the artisan nature of the people who lived in the area.

Trafalgar Street – The Great Eastern (still existing), The Beehive and the Coachman's Arms

Ann Street – Same Old House, Mazeppa Inn

London Street – The City of London

Elder Street – Rose & Crown and the Old Hoss.

New England Street – Merrie Harriers, Five Bells, the New England Inn (still existing but called the Cobbler's Thumb).

York Road North/York Hill – White Hart, the Brown Jug, the Fitter's Arms

Scandal

The oldest pub in the area, the Nag's Head, was reported in the Brighton Gazette of June 1851 for gambling offences.

> In December 1850 there was a dispute over gambling money owed involving cribbage, spinning jenny and nine pins. The gambling between four people went on to 2.00 am on one occasion and all night on another. One of the gamblers was a

licensed hawker with gold and silver and bottles of wine used as wagers with two of the gamblers being set up by the others. The judge gave a verdict in favour of the defendant who had lost all his money in the scam and said he would 'bare the name of the Nag's Head in remembrance'. In spite of this, the landlord, Mr. Thornton, remained at the pub until 1856.

Brighton Gazette 1851

The Druid's Arms outing c1930s. The pub was extended in the 1960s

The Nag's Head was one of the earliest pubs in the London Road area, serving as a stopping off point for early stage coaches

My grandfather Alfred James Elms, landlord of the Nag's Head pub, Queen's Place from 1898-1900, lost his licence for selling beer after hours through a hatch in the pavement.

Mr. A Elms

Walter Charles Gidney – a cripple, lost his licence after 15 years at the Mazeppa Inn, Ann Street, for contravening the Betting Act. The premise was extensively used for betting purposes. Men used to congregate daily at the house to discuss horse racing matters … they gave the landlord slips or verbal messages and he telephoned bets to a bookmaker. The house had been under observation for four days and then raided. £5 fine plus £2 costs.

Brighton & Hove Herald 16-7-1926

When we lived in New England Street we lived opposite the Merrie Harriers and every Bank Holiday there would be a beano organised by the publicans, Mr. & Mrs Carmichael. Men and women would have separate outings and all the kids would hang around trying to collect the coppers that were thrown from the back of the open charabanc. If our parents weren't in when we got home we would always go to look for them in the pub.

There were some characters in the area. There was Mrs. H who always sat in the private bar and ate her cheese roll that she had bought with her. Another old lady, who lived at the top of New England Street, always wore a long dress and when she left the pub would pee over a drain, much to the merriment of all the children.

Dolly Attrill

My parents met in The City of London pub in London Street. My dad was carrying a large bunch of flowers for his mother when he entered the pub. He caught mum's eye, went over to her and gave her one of the flowers. She had expected him to give her the whole bunch and was rather disgruntled at the time but she obviously forgave him, as they were married a year later. The City of London celebrated the Festival of Britain in 1951 by organising a street party. Everyone joined in with sandwiches, cake, jelly and blancmange for the children. Bunting was hung everywhere and there was a great atmosphere.

Marilyn Baker

I was born in 1922 and lived in the Elephant & Castle public house at 113 London Road until 1947/8. It had originally been a livery stable and coaching inn and was larger than some of the other local pubs. It had three bars, a large public bar, whose clientele was largely working class, many from the open market that was practically next-door. Mr. Dawkins the blacksmith used to be one of our customers, as was the Herbalist who had a stall next door to the blacksmiths. He wasn't a herbalist as we know them today; it was almost magic with demonstrations with a skull and flames. Darts and shove halfpenny were played in the public bar. There was a very small bottle and jug that didn't do much business and was already going out of fashion. It was little old ladies who came and sat on the bench or the old bentwood chairs who mainly frequented it. There were slightly posher people in the saloon bar where there was the only soft seating and the prices were slightly higher. The only food we served was bread, cheese and pickle, meat pies, biscuits and crisps.

The pub was an old building with four rooms in the attic that may have been used for accommodation at one time. There was a clubroom on the first floor that contained a ¾ size billiard table. This room was let out on various nights to different organizations e.g. the Mitre Cycling Club, Prestonville Nomads, Volunteers (an ex-army group) and a Dramatic Society. The pub would seem terribly bleak by modern standards. It was mainly varnished timber and above that embossed wallpaper painted green. There were beautiful mahogany counter tops that my father kept meticulously clean, and brass which was polished every week until it shone.

Then there were the spittoons that were lined with zinc and filled with fresh sawdust and emptied every day. There was a small spittoon in the saloon bar at first but we soon got rid of that but the one in the public bar remained until we left. At the end this wasn't used but it had been an acceptable habit with the working class at one time.

Saturday evenings were always the busiest time and we had to get an additional person in to wash the glasses but when I was big enough I helped in the kitchen. We had a 'maid of all work' who lived in. She came to live with us when I was 2 months old and stayed with us until we left the pub, so she was like one of the family. She was also a nurse and a lovely person; I was very fond of her. My parents ran a 'Tontine Club' that enabled people to save for Christmas but I don't remember anything else. I think they made a reasonable living although it was just a day-to-day pub. I didn't work in the pub myself until I came back from the army and saw that my parents were ailing and I had to practically run the pub until they retired.

Barry Leahy

When I worked in London Road I used the local pubs at lunchtime. The Shepherd & Dog was fairly old fashioned and it was mainly local workers who used it for a pint and a sandwich. The Bat & Ball had a landlord called Mr. Caldicott who was ex-army. Many working people who got in there at lunchtime came from the Labour Trades Club. Every Good Friday the Lewes Road working men's club fielded a team to play 'Bat & Trap' on the Level. The pub sign shows the game being played. The Elephant & Castle had a nice circular bar and it looked beautiful and was usually very busy with traders from the Open Market. The Mechanic's Arms was on the corner of Oxford Street and next door was a little pub called the Duke of Connaught. This was a brewery pub with green tiles on the outside, just like the Rose Hill Tavern. It had a bar window that opened onto the street. One card school regularly banned from the bar, stood in the street and played cards through the window onto a table pushed against the wall.

Eric Nicholls

**Built in 1901, the original Fire and Police House at Preston Circus
is being demolished to make way for the new Fire Headquarters built in 1939**

An early picture of the Brighton Fire Crew and dog ready for action c1920s

From Brewery to Fire Station

In 1901 a headquarters was built to co-ordinate the work of the twelve police and fire stations distributed around the town. It was erected on the site of the Amber Ale Brewery at Preston Circus. This site may have been considered suitable because of the natural supply of water from the Wellsbourne that ran from Patcham to the sea, although the geographic access to both north/south and east/west roads may have been a more important factor.

The appliances used at this time comprised of both horses and hand drawn escapes with manual and steam pumps. In 1910 bells were installed in every fireman's house enabling them to be 'on call' and a street fire alarm system was installed.

In 1921, the Town Council took the decision to re-organise and modernise the Fire Brigade. The Police and Volunteer Sections were disbanded and a professional Brigade was established with modern equipment.

The old headquarters at Preston Circus became inadequate for the needs of the Fire Brigade and in 1935, the Council approved plans for the erection of a new, larger fire station extended on the same site. Designed by Graeme Highet in Portland stone and brick, the new headquarters was opened by Earl Winterton on 21st May 1938.

On 1st April 1974, following the Local Government Act, the Brighton Fire Brigade became the responsibility of East Sussex County Council. In 2009 a possible relocation of the fire station is being considered.

Firemen Remember

Shortly after we moved to Chatham Place in 1933, the Fire Station had its annual display and mum took us kids to watch. The firemen were magnificent in their navy blue uniforms complete with belt, axe and brass helmets. They pitched their escape to the tower and performed rescues. They climbed hook ladders; the only thing between them and eternity was a steel hook that clipped over each windowsill. The grand finale was a fireman jumping into a special sheet held by his comrades. As we went home my mother asked me if I wanted to be a fireman. I gave the answer made famous in Pygmalion. Fate must have giggled some years later after my army demob, when I climbed into the same blue uniform and began 30 years service, albeit in the County Fire Brigade a few miles up the road.

David Huggins

I started as a fire cadet at the age of 16 and then 2 years later went to the training school at Roedean for twelve weeks and then returned to Brighton. The fire chief was Edmond Calvert who was quite an important person in town and sat on the Watch Committee and would censure what films we would see. He was a great theatre-goer and he would often bring the stars from various shows at the Theatre Royal back to the station for dinner. There would be outside caterers and he would ask the stars for their signatures which went on wall plaques.

The top floor of the Fire Station originally contained five 2/3 bedroomed flats for serving officers. Flat 6 was then the photographic department and the back of the flats had an open balcony that overlooked the station yard. When officers started buying their own houses the floor was knocked through and made into an office. It became the Fire Safety Office for many years.

I stayed at Brighton for ten years and in those days it was like a club. I can remember everyone's name and nickname. There was a lot of mickey-taking but it was like a big family really. If anyone was in trouble they were all there and I still see some of them socially. We worked on shifts, 3 days duty, 3 nights duty and 3 days off. Day duty was 9-6 pm and we'd all parade for inspection of uniform, check the inventory and then go through a test run. We'd check all the equipment on one of the 3 fire engines and go down London Road to St. Peter's church up Ditchling Road and down Beaconsfield Road to return back to the Fire Station. Then we would have a full scale drill and fix the ladders to the tower jets, water and so on. Then there was more cleaning and drilling for the younger firemen. Then in the afternoon we would check fire hydrants and water supplies. We would also do 'risk visits' by going to big hospitals etc. to look round, so in case of fire we knew what to do. The night shift started with the same procedure but then we would attend lectures e.g. topography and we all had to be trained in first aid. At 8.30 pm it was stand down time and we had recreational activities and at 11 pm it was heads down on camp beds.

Brighton was a very busy station and we rarely had a peaceful night. Friday and Saturday nights were the busiest nights because we had to board up all the broken windows that had been smashed in the town. They don't do that now, as they have to call out a glazier. Chimney fires were also a big problem then. Two of the worst fires I went to were possibly Johnson's store in Western Road and Bevan Funnell in Queen's Road.

If we were still sleeping at 6.30 am we would wake up, breakfast, clean up and then go home. On our off days we all had part-time jobs and I used to clean windows with a friend. In April 1964, six months after I became a fireman, we were working in Hollingbury and a lady who knew we were firemen came out and said 'Do you know there's a big fire in Brighton, one of the hotels is on fire.' By this time we could hear the sirens and see the smoke, so we packed up and rushed in my car to the fire station. There were no engines, so we were sent in my VW Beetle to the Bedford Hotel on the seafront and that was my first big fire. Brighton was originally the Borough Fire Brigade but we were amalgamated with East Sussex and Headquarters were moved to Lewes and they are now at Eastbourne.'

David Drew-Bear

The Duke of York's Picture Theatre

The Duke of York's Cinema is the oldest surviving purpose-built cinema in Britain. Now a Grade 2 listed building, it has been in almost continuous use as a cinema since it first opened on 22nd September 1910. It was built on the site of the Amber Ale Brewery, previously known as Longhurst's Brewery, at Preston Circus. It has an impressive frontage and the architects, Clayton & Black, created the elliptically curved ceiling that still survives today, as well as the arch and stage. The balcony was supported by columns with two boxes, one each side of the balcony.

The cinema was formally opened under the name 'The Duke of York's Picture Theatre' by the Mayor of Brighton, Charles Thomas Stanford. Mrs. Violet Melnotte-Wyatt, the owner, was also the proprietor of the Duke of York's Theatre in London, and using the same name as the theatre for her new cinema also coincided with the accession of George Vth, Duke of York. The cinema cost £3,000 to build and had a carpeted auditorium with 800 tip up seats, air conditioning by electric fan and the largest projection room in Brighton. Original ticket prices ranged from 3d, 6d, and 1s to 2s 6d for the boxes.

In 1918 the cinema was sold to Jack Channon of Sussex Picturedromes and in 1930 a sound system was installed. The first talkie to be shown is believed to have been 'The Jazz Singer' starring Al Jolson. The cinema closed on June 21st 1937 for refurbishment, reopening a week later with seat numbers reduced to 750. In 1946 there were further improvements with new Kalee projectors and British Thomson-Houston sound system installed. By 1948 the ticket prices ranged from 7d to 2s 3d and in 1953 they had risen to 9d to 2s 6d. In February 1956 there was the first screening of the newly installed Cinemascope with a 28 ft x 12 ft screen.

In the early 1960s, under the management of Peter Drew-Bear, the programmes were changed three times a week but by the 1970s the cinema was also being used for bingo and it looked as if it would go the way of many of the other cinemas in Brighton and close.

The Duke of York's Picture Theatre c1924

After several new owners during the 1970s the 'Dukes' began a partial 'art-house' programme following the closure of the Brighton Film Theatre in North Street. After a short closure the cinema reopened in October 1981 under the new management of Rosier Films who had acquired it for £50,000. In 1983 another new owner, the Penultimate Picture Palace Company, refurbished the cinema reducing the seating to 302.

In October 1994 the cinema was acquired by City Screen and run as part of the Picturehouse Cinema circuit, showing art-house, classic and some first-run films with children's and silver screen programmes. It is also the venue for local film festivals and now offers Autism-Friendly Screenings and special events.

In 2010 the Duke of York's cinema plans a celebratory year of events to mark 100 years of the Duke of York's with a community–led research project to create an online 'virtual museum' dedicated to its history.

My father, Peter Drew-Bear, was a projectionist at the Duke of York's cinema from the early to mid 50's. Mrs Bradshaw, who had owned the cinema for some years, employed my father as the manager of the cinema from about 1957. She then decided to sell it and my father bought it and ran the Duke's from 1967 -75. When he first took over it was quite run down and he bought loads of seats, several new screens and new projectors. Off duty firemen painted the cinema.

The cinema had been built on the site of the Amber Brewery and at that time you could still see the vents of the hop room if you walked along Stanley Road. You could also still smell the hops, especially in the roof space and we would have to frequently clear that out.

I can remember crowds queuing right round Stanley Road past the Fire Station entrance. My father said that people used to turn up and pay their entrance money and then ask what the film was. They didn't go to see the film it was just to go to the cinema. I can remember watching Edgar Lustgarten crime films, adverts, the news and the big film, so you really got value for money.

The sweet shop was on the right as you entered and it also had a front opening for passing trade. My father used to stand outside and if he could see somebody coming one hundred yards away he'd shout 'There's somebody coming.' He'd love rainy weather, especially on Saturday and Sunday when you couldn't move for crowds. All day people would come in with their sandwiches and some even brought their babies with them. My father stood out at the front of the house in his dinner suit. There was also a doorman called Bill Hillman who wore a Commissionaire's outfit in red and black with a peaked cap. He used to have a little fellow with him called Tom who was also in uniform. Tom was disabled and became part of the furnishings and he always came to us for Christmas dinner. It was Tom's job to stoke the boilers and he was always told to heat them up in the summer in order to sell more ice creams.

Mabel, who had originally played the piano for the silent movies, was the cashier in the 50s and she sat between the doors with the clock above her – she was very strict. Later my stepmother Jean used to take the money and worked in the sweet shop. If you've ever seen 'The Smallest Show on Earth' that was the 'Dukes'.

In the old days (before I knew the cinema) the firemen who were on 24 hour watch used to go to the cinema and they had a bell system at the back of the cinema that would warn them when the fire bell went off. They would sit there in the back rows and they would all leave through the sweet shop door when the fire bell went off.

The cinema also had double seats in both the balcony and downstairs and these were very popular with couples. Every year at Christmas, my father would collect presents donated by the cinema-goers to take to an orphanage on Christmas Day. I would accompany him along with the Commissionaire. During the 70s cinema numbers dropped, possibly because of the growth of the video market. My father couldn't get the top films and in those days you actually bought some of the films. These would be used again and again, films like 'The Magnificent Seven' or Midnight Cowboy' and these always guaranteed a crowd, but it wasn't enough. My father tried to run Bingo evenings but he didn't have wrestling or strip shows, as some books have quoted. He could have kept it going if he'd had a grant but these weren't available then.

The university students have made a difference to cinemas like the 'Dukes' that show less commercial films. It's good to see that the cinema is still going and they've kept it well. I believe it's the oldest purpose-built cinema still in use today.

David Drew-Bear

My family moved to 59 Clyde Road in 1912. Every Saturday afternoon there was a special children's show at the Duke of York's cinema that cost 1d. We would arrive clutching our pennies to find it was packed with children and we loved it. There was a lady on the platform playing the piano because they were silent films then. When we started all the children roared out the song that ended 'God bless the Prince of Wales'. We would then sit back and enjoy the films, all the children laughing and shouting.

Hilda Barber

A view of the Duke of York's looking towards Stanley & Clyde Roads

Churches & Chapels

St. Bartholomew's Church

The Rev Arthur Douglas Wagner, perpetual Curate of St Paul's Brighton and son of the Vicar of Brighton, Henry Wagner, was a follower of the Oxford movement within the Church of England. Aside from the religious aspect of this movement, it advocated taking religion to the working people and accordingly with money inherited from his aunt, Arthur Wagner set about building churches in the poorer areas of Brighton.

The original church of St Bartholomew was built in 1868 in a small corner of Jackson's Field in Providence Place, one of the last remaining spare pieces of land in the area. It was a small mission church built of brick and rubble to seat 350 people. In 1871, Wagner built a school alongside this church for the railway workers children, designed in Gothic style by Edmund Scott and built by a local builder, Stenning and Sons. Both these institutions were well patronised to the extent that Wagner bought the rest of Jackson's field to build a much larger church. The design by Edmund Scott showed one long nave with no apse, and would abut the school building giving it a combined length of 322 feet. Part of the existing church of 1868 would have needed to be demolished.

Wagner was not happy with this proposal, wanting to keep the original church intact. He felt that the proposed height of the new building, of 80 feet, was insignificant. The plans were amended in 1873, even though the foundations had been laid in February 1872, and oral consent was allegedly given by the local planners. The church was opened on 8 September 1874, and was 135 feet in height, with 9 buttresses, and this immediately provoked an angry town council debate about flouting planning permission but when it was realised that Wagner could only be fined 42 shillings on a building costing £18,000, the matter was dropped. The building was one immense nave, very plain in decor, relief being given to the stark brick walls by the patterns created by the use of mixed stocks of brick. Above the altar was a huge crucifix composed of tiles incised by an encaustic process, designed by S. Bell, who also designed the painted panels of the high altar.

During the period 1895 to 1910, under the auspices of the Vicar, Arthur Cocks, a supporter of the Arts and Craft Workers Guild, the church was beautified by the creation of a huge marble baldachino (altar canopy) designed by Henry Wilson. Wilson was a follower of Lethaby, an expert on Byzantine art and he put in place a marble pulpit and font, and an art nouveau style Lady Altar in silver. Although Wilson's plans were never completed, including an extension which would have required demolition of the school and the original church, the Sanctuary was enhanced by Italian style mosaics in 1915. The building and decor has made it a Grade 1 listed building. Plans to extend the church in 1930 to designs by Sir Giles Gilbert Scott were thwarted by the need to re-slate the roof.

The church was immensely successful with the workers of the area and the wealthier population of Brighton who particularly liked the style of worship and choral services. Two notable incumbents were Canon Dilworth Harrison and Canon Hutchinson in the 1930s and 1950s who often petitioned the local council on behalf of the poor. The church ran working men's clubs, a small theatre, and had nuns serving the church from mission houses in the area in London Road, Beaconsfield Road, Rose Hill Terrace and Ditchling Rise giving out food and clothing to those in need in the parish

St. Bartholomew's Parochial Excursion to Burgess Hill on June 25th 1908

The Anglo-Catholic Congress in 1922
The Bishop of Lewes leads the procession along London Road, turning into Ann Street

Methodism

After the building of Dorset Gardens Wesleyan Methodist Chapel in1808, all of the different branches of Methodism in Brighton built their first chapels in Kemp Town. It was not until the late 1860s that Methodist chapels were built outside that area.

The first such chapel belonged to the United Methodist Church (UMFC) when a few people broke away from Dorset Gardens. They met in hired rooms but after a few weeks the London Brighton & South Coast Railway (LBSCR) let them use a reading room at its works. By 1867 the small society had grown sufficiently to be able to build its own chapel. This was built on land leased from the LBSCR at 27 Ann Street, on the corner of Queen Street and was known as the Queen Street Chapel. Very few records survived but the Trust deed shows that of the ten trustees who lived in Brighton no fewer than seven had occupations like 'engineer' that associated them with the LBSCR. The UMFC in Brighton did not last very long and by 1885 the Chapel had been leased by the LBSCR to the Wesleyan Methodists for 25 years at 5 shillings p.a. However, in 1903 the railway company needed the land for 'a heavy programme of extensions', and the Chapel closed with most members joining other Wesleyan Methodist congregations.

The Primitive Methodists had a slow start in Brighton. Their strength nationally lay in close-knit communities such as mining, agricultural and fishing. It was not until the development of the railway, especially the engineering works in the later part of the 19th century that they were able to grow and establish themselves in Brighton. By 1891 there were 2,651 people employed at the railway works and there also references to a 'railway mission' in Viaduct Road at this time, but this is a misnomer. The Viaduct Road Primitive Methodist Chapel was opened in 1876 and was only known as the 'railway mission' after it was sold by the Primitive Methodists in 1894 when they moved to their new chapel in London Road. In the period 1875-1900 those connected with the railway provided the largest group of families (20%) who had Primitive Methodist baptisms, easily outnumbering those whose fathers were described as 'labourers'.

The minister, the Rev. William Dinnick, had always intended to build a chapel in London Road and, confusingly, the Viaduct Road Primitive Methodist Chapel was called the London Road Chapel. Dinnick arrived in Brighton in 1876 and stayed until his death in 1901. This was very unusual as most ministers in all branches of Methodism moved around every few years. When Dinnick died it was commented that his 25 year pastorate was, at that time, the longest continuous one anywhere in the world of Methodism.

Also most unusual was the method of financing the Primitive Methodist chapels in Brighton under Dinnick. The last part of the 19th century in Brighton saw much contention between the 'catholic' wing of the Church of England, for example St. Bartholomew's Church, and those who saw this movement as leading inexorably to the Roman Catholic Church, then viewed with a horror that we find difficult to appreciate now. Some Anglicans saw Primitive Methodism in Brighton as a means by which the working class could be kept from the Anglo-Catholics. For example T.A. Denny of London, describing himself as a 'Churchman', gave £150 for the building of the Viaduct Road Primitive Methodist Church, 'to counteract the evils of Romanism, Superstition, Infidelity and other sins …' Anglicans were not the only supporters; the Treasurer of the appeal to raise money for the Viaduct Road Chapel was G. F. Tippett, a local Congregationalist. In 1895 at one of the open events for the London Road Chapel Alderman Martin remarked that 'the bright and happy faces of Christian souls was all the decoration truly needed.' This was presumably meant as a contrast to St. Bartholomew's.

The London Road Primitive Methodist Chapel involved itself fully in the life of the local community. To the traditional activities of Sunday School, weekday meetings, and a range of musical events, were added activities such as the Slate Club to help people in time of sickness. By the time the Slate Club closed in 1972 there had been over 1,100 members (597 women and 511 men): the large majority of who cannot have been members of the Church.

The church hall in London Road was used as a 'British Restaurant' during WW11, serving about 250 meals a day. The Church underwent major rebuilding in the early 1950s when the present façade was built. However, the population was moving away from the area and this was one of the reasons for the Scout Troop having to disband in the late 1950s. In 1973 there was a proposal to close this and other small Methodist churches in central Brighton and join Stanford Avenue but it was not followed through. Eventually the declining membership, few of whom now lived in the area, meant that the decision was taken by the Church Council to close the Church and the last service was held in 2006, thereby ending a period of over 125 years of Methodist presence and service in the area.

London Road Congregational Church (1830-1958) in 1964, just before demolition.
The north side of Ann Street, above St. Peter's Street,
has already been demolished and is being used as a car park

The Viaduct Rd. Primitive Methodist Chapel opened in 1876
The chapel is now known as the Calvary Evangelical Church

This 1961 panoramic view across the demolition site shows
the New England Road Mission Church demolished in the 1990s

The photograph, taken c1925, is of Marshall's Row from the London Road end
The houses were built by John Marshall c1750s and demolished by 1938 to allow The Open Market to extend

The Battle for the Open Market

A sign at the Ditchling Road end of the market states 'Welcome to the Open Market – Established during 1920s.' This is not quite correct and certainly does not reflect the pain of its true origins.

Whilst some traders claim that Harry Cowley started the Market in 1919, it appears from his own comments that it had generated spontaneously during the First World War by ex Servicemen. He talked about the battle of the Oxford Street market, 'It was a wartime market and the boys had the order of the boot.' It was 1919 and Harry and his friend Alf Richardson set about preventing the closure of the market. Having set up a rostrum in London Road, across the tram tracks, Harry soon gathered a crowd. The authorities responded by sending two trams full of police to the barricade, and approaching it, they drew truncheons and attacked. "Stick it Alf", said Harry, who then stayed on the rostrum throughout the police raid. By doing so Harry eventually got a promise from the authorities that the market situation would be reviewed. In 1921, the market was moved from Oxford Street to the Level and stretched along the path on the north side beside Union Road. The Market comprised a mixture of former barrow boys and those, without employment, who wanted to start up a trade but could not afford the rent for a shop.

For many traders it was the family who assisted them in setting up. One ex-trader said: 'My father started his stall with a £10 loan from his sister, and set up a fish stall', a business that was to continue until the mid 1960s. Similarly, Doris Watherington (nee Mitchell), recalls that her grandfather George James Mitchell (a fisherman and boatman known on the beach as Old Ball Mitchell) gave money to one of his sons, John 'Shrimp' Mitchell to set up his fishmongers stall, located towards the Elm Grove end of the market and close to his home in Park Crescent. Eventually each of Shrimp Mitchell's sons, Bill, Joe, and Jack Mitchell, all had stalls in the market. Jack Mitchell's stall carried the name JACK MITCHEL, which arose, according to his son Robert who managed the stall into the 1990s, because he didn't leave enough room on the board for the last L!

Johnnie Stevens (greengrocer) and Mr Harding (fishmonger) both started in the market from being barrow boys. After leaving school in 1918, Mr Harding started in the Oxford Street market with his father, an ex-Navy man. Before the market moved to the Level the council did not charge for the stalls. They got all their fish from Brighton Fish Market and were well known and trusted enough to buy on credit, paying the suppliers at the end of each week. As the stall became more successful, it was enlarged.

In 1926, the market moved from the Level to spare land between the rear of houses in Francis Street and the front gardens of houses in Marshall's Row. It was thought that the Open Market was at one time located in the Market Hall sited in Ann Street. However, one retired trader recalled that this was not the case. There was a similar market held under cover in Ann Street, close to Providence Place and behind what is now Ransom's shop, but it was separate from the Open Market. Indeed, one of the trader's relatives had a stall in the Ann Street market hall, which in the 1870s had been part of an engine works, and in the 1950s it had become part of the depot for Parson's paints.

Getting goods into the Marshall's Row site, as it originally stood, was not easy.

Most produce was brought to the London Road end by wholesalers' lorries, and stallholders hired handcarts from Dawkin's Forge for three pence a day to take their produce from the entrance to the stall. This practice carried on until 1938, when the houses in Marshall's Row were demolished and the market expanded over the area, with some space being left so that the wholesalers' lorries could get right into the market area, behind the stalls.

A Market Trader

By the 1930s there were up to nine fishmongers in the Open Market, a trader recalled the names as if it were yesterday, 'Kelly's, Marmery's, Taylor's, Burgess's, Harding's, Cyril Rolf, Shrimp Mitchell (later run by his sons Joe, Fred, and Dennis), John Mitchell (trading as Jack Mitchel), and Bill Mitchell.' Johnnie Stevens was recalled as being one of the traders and was adjacent to Burgess's fish stall 'he had the finest show of fruit and vegetables in Brighton.'

The market community was strong in many senses, it could operate almost like an extended family and yet life was hard and at times the harshness seemed to overrule the community spirit.

> I remember Topper, he was an old man who rented his stall and, despite making a living, he would sleep rough, frequently in the doorway of Champion's pram shop in Baker Street, just above the market. On Fridays many traders went for a fish supper in 'Ibbotson's' in Baker Street (now Bardsley's) and Topper was often treated to a supper. Topper eventually caught frostbite, his health deteriorated rapidly and he died. Despite being well known in the market, I was the only trader to attend his funeral.

A Market Trader

Fridays and Saturdays were the main days for the Market.

> It was 'chock a block'. Sometimes you had to close the stall because of the queue, and leave for ten or twenty minutes. But when you got back, the people who were at the front of the queue when you left, would still be there wanting to be served. Most traders liked a drink or two and at the quieter moments would go to the 'Oxford Arms' in Oxford Street, or if they wanted somewhere a bit posh or private to the 'Elephant and Castle' in London Road.

A Market Trader

The market was divided to some extent by the produce sold. Second hand furniture was towards the London Road end, whilst greengrocery and fishmongers were at the Ditchling Road end adjacent to Woods tobacconist shop. A fishmonger recalled that

during the war they had to belong to the Fishmongers Federation to qualify for the supply of the limited fish available under the rationing scheme in operation. It was mainly at this time that the fish supplies were obtained from beyond Brighton Fish Market, from Rye, Dungeness and even beyond.

The Market remained as a wood and corrugated iron structure on each side of what had been Marshall's Row and the earlier vacant site until 1963. In that year, the Council decided that it had to be rebuilt to conform to modern Health and Safety rules. Half the market was cleared at a time, and the current brick built stalls were erected, then they did the other half, squashing the temporary stalls up into each half in turn. Recently, an awning style roof was erected, but with only part success in terms of providing shelter, and in attempting to modernise the appearance of the market. It is the view of some that as Health and Safety standards are tightened, that the really long term outlook for the Open Market is not secure, but it remains as a symbol of defiance of authority in those difficult and harsh days of First World War Brighton.

My mother always used the Open Market for her vegetables, most of the local people did. As you came in from the Level there was a blind man on the left corner. He sold cheap toys and if we'd done odd errands and we'd saved a few pennies it was quite a treat to go to his stall on a Saturday.

David Guildford

As a boy in the 1930s I had a job working for Price's Bakery in Coombe Road. All deliveries were then made using a horse and cart and it was my job to take the horses to Dawkin's Forge for shoeing. There were four horses Jack, Polly, Sandy & Bob and every week I would take one horse to be shod. Mr. Agar made sure that I could ride with a saddle and I'd ride from Coombe Road to the forge at the Open Market. I'd wait until the horse had been shod and then ride back. Health & Safety wouldn't allow it now. Jack was a big powerful horse and during the war I was returning with him along Union Road when a bomber passed overhead and Jack bolted. I was really scared and it nearly stopped me doing the job again but I did continue. In about 1947 there was a transition from horse drawn carts to electric floats, so my journeys to the forge ceased.

Peter Llewellyn

Marshall's Row in the 1950s after the removal of the cottages

The market was very different then with open stalls built of canvas on wire frames and wooden counters. Saturday night was good for bargains, but I especially remember Christmas. Christmas Eve arrived and it was time to buy the meat we would eat for our Christmas dinner. Turkey and chicken were for the well off in those days, for us it was a choice of pork, beef or lamb. Late Christmas Eve we would go to the Open Market knowing full well that the later it got the more desperate the butchers would be to sell their meat. These were the days before freezers and the meat was just hung up on hooks. The trick with the women was to know when to shout yes. I used to go with my mum and stand under the gas flares lighting the market and get more and more desperate, as she appeared to miss all the bargains. She knew exactly when to shout and would get so much for her money that we would have a job struggling home with it. One year the butcher got so mad with mum he took off his striped apron and threw it at her shouting 'You might as well have the blankety blank shop as well.' She countered with 'Throw in your straw hat and it's a deal.

We never went to the market without a visit to the forge. We loved its brightly glowing fire pumped up by the bellows and the clang of the hammer on hot metal with all its resulting sparks.

David Huggins

One of the last photos of Dawkin's Forge before its demolition in the 1960s

Brighton Co-operative Society

'Unity is Strength'

The first property the Society bought in London Road was number 96, a house owned by Mrs. Glaisyer costing £2,000. This was the beginning of the Co-op coming 'out of the side streets and into the high street.' The Registered Office was transferred to this address from North Road and the first meeting was held there on July 17th 1906. In 1908 they purchased No. 97 and 98 (Wm.White furniture dealer), in 1909 No. 99 (H. Dudman, masseur and surgical rubber) and No.100 the home of John Brown. In 1909 the lease of 101 was bought for £1,000, so in six years, the Society had acquired the nucleus of the site for around £6,500.

In 1910 alterations and additions were carried out at Nos 99, 100 and 101. Nos. 99-100 became the Drapery & Millinery department and Nos. 97 & 98 the Boot & Shoe department. By 1921 three more properties Nos 95, 112 and 113 had also been acquired.

Between 1929 and 1931 these smaller shops were replaced by a new building. Built in a Neo-classical style it was light and airy, achieving size and scale without piling mass on mass. Designed by Bethell & Swannell, it had four storeys and 180 ft. frontage. Additions were later made both at the front of the store and in Baker Street, where the Society gradually acquired sites for the extension. In 1956 there were plans for future development to build a food hall on the site of the Society properties at 84, 85 and 86 London Road, close to the central premises.

In 1960 proposals for a new food hall were made for the Baker Street site and this was opened on 22nd September 1962. In the 1970s there were further plans for a massive extension to form a supermarket of 6,500 sq. ft. on the ground floor and space for a non-food department on the first floor. In January 1974 this was refused on the grounds that housing accommodation would be lost in Kingsbury Street. It took several years to eventually obtain the planning permission required, the supermarket finally opening on 20th May 1980.

The Co-op, with its fair prices and half yearly dividend payments had played an important role in the lives of ordinary working families in Brighton. In the 1980s shopping habits began to change and the Co-op, once the largest department store in Brighton, found it more difficult to compete. Gradually more internal shop space was leased to outside firms and it was with regret that the announcement was made in 2006 that the store would cease trading in February 2007, leaving only the supermarket in Baker Street still functioning.

It was with great sadness that many people visited the Co-op during its last weeks of trading when even the internal fixture and fittings were being sold. This beautiful building now stands empty in London Road, except for a Post Office counter, a ghost of its former glory as 'The People's Business'.

> I sometimes helped my older brother on his Co-op milk round. The horses and floats would line up in London Terrace at the rear of the Co-op store in London Road ready to start the rounds. There was a uniformity and smartness of the men, many who had just returned from fighting in the Great War. They had large milk urns on their carts which were the property of the Co-op and were exchanged daily. Many customers

In 1906 the Co-operative Society bought 96 London Road
and established a retail history that lasted for over 100 years

Designed by Bethel & Swannell in a Neo-classical style,
the new Co-op building opened in 1931

had their own milk cans and they would be filled daily according to the customer's requirements. The cans were left outside the front door hanging from a hook, as bottles did not come into circulation until 1924. The horses knew the rounds better than the milkman. It was known that milkmen could be offered drinks on Christmas Eve and the horse would be responsible for getting them home. They changed to motorised floats c1960 and the stable manager worked hard to get all the horses new homes.

Frank Edwards

I started working for the Co-op straight from school in the late 30s. I was an office boy at first and delivered letters and notes daily to all the local branches by bike. When I first started we had compulsory fire watching. I was only getting 25/- a week but if you went fire watching from 8 pm – 7 am we got an extra 2/6d. We had camp beds in the boardroom with a blimming big clock that went 'clonk' every half hour. During the war the staff were all young, old or married women. Way back it didn't matter who you worked for: Marks, Boots or the Co-op, you were a member of the family whether you were a lowly office boy or a shop manager. There was a canteen on the top floor, you had to pay but you could get bread and jam or bread and dripping, as well as hot meals. Males and females had separate rooms, you didn't sit together then but then they changed all that. That's why there are so many couples working for the Co-op that married.

All the shops in London Road and North Street used to shut on Thursday afternoon. For staff working in the shops it was the only opportunity they had to get together and court. They didn't meet most of the world's population. We worked from 9-5.30 pm with one and a quarter hours for lunch but pre war we did a 48 hour week and opened late Friday & Saturday.

I went to the share office with Mr. Packham and he was a gentleman. There were still managers who 'ruled the roost' and if you upset them they could get nasty. There used to be pneumatic tubes that went right to the top floor with the money and the change and receipt used to be sent back. In the 1930s the Co-op had huge factories and most of their products were made by the Co-op themselves.

Dennis & Marjorie Andrews

I went with my mother to the Co-op store in London Road to apply for a job as a shoe repairer. The interview was held in an office under the stairs where a man with a winged collar was sitting. My mother sat in the only chair that could be squeezed in and that's how I started. The job wasn't very well paid but there was a pension scheme that my father thought was wonderful. I was quite good at football and I had been offered a job with Tottenham Hotspurs but my father said that with the Co-op I'd have a job for life. The Co-op building looked very impressive and had a strict standard of behaviour expected from its staff and I felt proud to work there.

During my first days there I realised that everyone else was disabled. The men who worked there had shoes with metal straps going up the sides, large boots, loss of fingers and thumbs and a humped back. I wondered why a 14 year old boy was working in a place like this but I think the Co-op was very sympathetic to those who were handicapped. I was taught by Mr. Collins who took me through the whole process of making shoes. He taught me not to put the rivets in my mouth but in the palm of my hand and flick them onto my finger. This was so I didn't get black teeth or lips from the metal.

I found the Co-op a good firm to work for, as they were considerate about their staff. One day a week they sent me to a class at Coombe Road school for 'Citizenship' lessons which was absolutely brilliant for somebody who had a interrupted education because of the war. We were taught things like letter writing, how to use the library, how to vote and money management. At the end of each class the class teacher would read from a book, usually a classic and I found this very stimulating. I learnt the trade and returned to work at the Co-op after National Service but I felt unsettled. I eventually left but I have very fond memories of working at the Co-op and the opportunity it gave me to extend my education.

Stanley Wilson

I left school in March 1938 and I started my first job at the Co-op in April of that year. My mother and grandmother were ardent Co-op members and they chose the job for me. All 14 year olds started work in the cheque office for two years and then they were able to work for other offices. When you bought something in the Co-op you were given a cheque with a share number on it. The girls upstairs used to sort millions and millions of cheques and then enter them by machine, so that the dividends were available every 6 months. I was made a supervisor after two years and eventually had sixty staff under me at age 18 and received a 2/6d rise. I wanted to leave but my mother wouldn't let me, you didn't leave jobs in those days.

In 1963 they decided to modernise and did away with the cheque system and we became more mechanised and eventually I was trained on the computer. All the managers wore black pinstripe trousers and black coats with tails but Mr. Hesketh, he went the whole hog with a butterfly collar and a cravat. When they extended into Baker Street it was a nightmare. They took over the pork butchers on the corner, Catt's the newsagents and all the little shops up to London Terrace and the rebuilding took 18 months.

Peggy Turpin

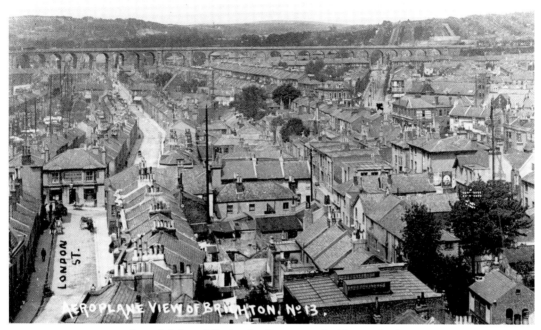

An aerial view of the London Street area looking north c1910
The pub facing London Street is the Phoenix Inn at 29 York Hill

Taken on 9-5-1949, this photo shows the beginning of the clearances
Footitt's greengrocer's shop was at 79 New England Street and Boston Street
faces the shunting line and embankment of the goods yard

Demolition – Demolition - Demolition!

Demolition and redevelopment have featured at regular intervals in Brighton. The method chosen for one of the earliest clearances was horrifying.

> The slums of Durham & Petty France (an area near the Clock Tower and the present Queen's Road) were demolished in 1845. The reasons did not stem from concern for the inhabitants, but because these slums were along the route from the station to the seafront, and the Town Commissioners did not wish the visitors to see them. Neither did they gain the consent of the tenants; the inhabitants … had to be lured out of their houses by a festivity at the cricket ground (the Level). While they were there, the houses were demolished.
>
> ***Town Commissioner's Report 1845***

In the London Road area the first act of demolition occurred in 1853, as part of the London Brighton and South Coast Railway Act of that year. In Cavendish Place North (see map) 28 houses were pulled down to extend the goods yard. No scheme existed at that time to rehouse the 189 displaced residents.

In 1897/98, the London Brighton and South Coast Railway (LBSCR) decided to further expand the goods yard, mainly for the coal trade. This required the compulsory purchase of houses in Belmont Place, Fleet Street, Queen Street, Peel Street, Peel Place, and parts of Ann Street, Boston Street, and the west side of New York Street. The LBSCR Act of 1898 permitted this, but required the company to comply with the Housing of the Working Classes Act of 1890, and provide alternative housing. In all 171 houses were demolished affecting nearly 1,000 people. The LBSCR paid owners an average of £430 per house although one owner occupier received £600 and public houses affected were purchased for £2,000 or more. The LBSCR built Inwood Crescent (originally called St. James' Crescent) and Compton Road on their land above Preston Park station to provide flats and houses for the displaced families, but it did not work out as planned. Knowing that there was the threat of demolition, people started to move out of the area before the new houses were built. Demolition was complete by 1904/05 but only three residents moved into these new houses. The houses in Boston Street, also purchased by the LBSCR for the project but never demolished, were an attractive alternative being nearby and cheaper to rent. There were objections to the scheme, in particular from Mepham's, whose bakery in Peel Place was affected, but they were overruled.

In 1925, the council cleared land in front of Marshall's Row to relocate the Open Market from the Level. In 1930, as part of a slum clearance, the houses in Marshall's Row were pulled down along with those in Oxford and Brunswick Courts, just off Oxford Street where the car park now exists. Here houses vied with a small abattoir for space in a blocked-off court and some houses had access only to communal privies. The council did nothing with the land: albeit small sections were sold off to Bellman's in London Road (now Boots and Somerfield), some to Buxton's in Ditchling Road and some to the Post Office. The Second World War brought such activity to an end, but after 1945, with councils required to have 5 year plans on housing needs, attention was drawn again to assessing sub standard housing and clearance of such areas. As a result of such activity, in 1955, the Boston Street, Wood Street & Blackman Street Compulsory Purchase Orders were made.

Why were these houses built in the 1850s selected for clearance whilst those of similar age in the Hanover area of Brighton remain to this day? The houses in Hanover tended to be slightly larger, commanded higher rents and were generally in a better state of repair. In the London Road area the house size and state did vary. Some in Boston Street/Cross Street and Elder Row had frontages of 12 feet or less, a depth of 20 feet and ceiling heights of 6 feet, with very enclosed, tiny backyards containing an outdoor toilet. With poor lighting, ventilation and crowded aspect, it was considered such houses were unfit for habitation. Those in Boston Street faced the elevated shunting line and embankment of the goods yard, whilst those in Elder Row opened out onto a narrow passage and the backyards of Elder Street. Bombing had damaged houses in Elder Place and in the surrounding area. While better houses did exist in the Compulsory Purchase Order area, isolating these for retention just did not make sense, and so the whole area was cleared by 1957. One of the last buildings to go was the Old Hoss beer house on the corner of Elder Street. In the main the council purchased the land on which these houses stood for £50 or less.

Around 1965/67 the third CPO area was declared for London Street, and included New York Street, Providence Place (including St Bartholomew's school), Ann Street, St Peter's Street and Belmont Street. There was an adverse reaction to the CPO in Belmont Street and one resident, Olive Young, did successfully pursue the council for improved compensation and obtained a market value for her house.

The clearance of Francis Street also occurred about this time, but this was to create space for the market traders and was not contained within a CPO although many of the houses in this street would have fallen into the unfit category. In 1966, the wartime prefabs in Viaduct Road were cleared. These homes, erected on a bombsite in 1944 as Brighton's first prefabs, were the last to be cleared from the town having long outlived their 10 year lifespan.

The lack of a strategic plan by the local authority meant that much of the area remained derelict for 40 years with some very haphazard rebuilding. The one outstanding building in terms of concepts was New England House. This flatted factory was seen as an innovation in 1960, built to house the many small workshops displaced by various clearance schemes. The high rents charged by the Council meant that it was not an initial success although one firm has occupied units in the building since it opened. It remains useful for its purpose but sadly unlikely to earn points for architectural merit. Over the years this clearance area has been the subject of grand plans like the Preston Circus relief road, and the Station to London Road shopping Centre with its proposed Westminster style Piazza in front of St Bartholomew's Church. Instead the area had been infilled with poor quality industrial sheds under the title of The Longley Industrial estate. Only now, 50 years after the CPO was issued, has the area been rebuilt. The New England Quarter, may at last breathe some new life into this much maligned and maltreated area.

When I was young, my family lived at 1 Cross Street and later 26 New England Street. My parents were Reg and Lou Salvage and there were four children. My father was a fisherman by trade and he worked with his older brother and shared a boat with others to catch mackerel or herring. He left home at 4 am every morning and walked to the seafront. My mother would meet them at 8 am with the fish cart and they would push it back through the small streets calling on their regular customers. They would have a pitch at the corner of New York Street, at the top of York Hill next to the 'Fitter's Arms' pub. Dad had a big slab that pulled in and out where he could fillet the fish and people asked for pieces for the cat.

When we lived at Cross Street in the 1920s, the rent man came round to collect the ten shillings rent. The house had two bedrooms, front room, kitchen and scullery. There was also a small yard that led into Boston Street where we kept the fish barrow. Nobody seemed to mind and it was never taken. Any fish that was left over would be stored in the back yard on a stone floor with a cover over it. It was kept wet by throwing buckets of fresh water on it.

We later moved to New England Street which had four bedrooms. My parents then kept their barrow in Elder Place where there was a big yard with horses but they had to pay to keep it there. When we were told we had to move we didn't really want to go as there was nothing wrong with the houses and we liked the friendly community. Everyone mucked in and helped each other, sometimes taking round a bucket of coal for the fire. If anyone became ill my mum would drop some fresh fish in for their meal. They offered us a house in Hollingdean but we didn't like it because it wasn't handy for the shops in London Road.

Dolly Attrill nee Salvage

We lived in Boston Street which was a very close-knit community and you did actually know everyone in the street. Our house was literally overlooked by the railway shunting shed. When I was a kid it seemed as if it was miles away but in fact it was very near our front door. There was a high stone wall and an embankment and the train would come in and turn on a turntable and would sometimes set light to the grass. Near our street there was a rag and bone man and he used to come round with a barrow collecting old clothes. We also had a whelk man on Sundays and a fish barrow twice a week and especially on Fridays. It was luxury to have a bit of fish. We had a small yard in which we had chickens and rabbits which were our food supply. Very rarely could you afford to go out and buy meat. Our dog (a cross Alsatian) used to take me to St. Barts school every day and on his way back he would stop at the butcher's shop and get himself a big marrow bone. He also met me from school in all weathers. Everyone loved the area and all our family lived near us. My parents rented their house and they were amongst the first to be moved. They started clearing the houses from the top (of the street), so members of the family all moved at different times. You were just offered a house and that was that, you didn't have a choice. I remember going to look at a house in Shortgate Road, Moulsecoomb with my mother and the next thing I knew we were packing. A few weeks afterwards my eldest sister took me back to see the houses being pulled down. All the people who had lived in the houses had turned up. It wasn't that sad for me because I was young but I know my sister was upset. I can remember a lot of the neighbours were crying because their community had gone.

David Guildford

My grandparents moved to No. 2 London Street in 1929 and my grandmother remained living there until 1963. The street contained small terraced houses and the 'City of London Inn'.

We entered the house directly from the street into a narrow hallway. On the right there was a front room which was used for weddings, christenings, funerals and Christmas only. The living room contained a table and chairs and that is where I remember Granny and Uncle Charlie spent most of their time. It was a very small room with lino on the floor and small mats scattered here and there to make the room seem warmer. Thick net curtains were at one window at the rear and beyond the nets was a dark blue roller blind. Granny would ask one of us to roll down the blind when the sun was setting to 'shut out the gloom.' The scullery contained an oblong shaped sink and a wooden table with just a cold water tap. Underneath the table there were two very large stone crocks for bread and flour. Meat and other perishable foods were kept in the meat safe which was on the wall in the pantry. Off the back of the scullery there was a small, very basic room where laundry was done with a gas powered copper. The toilet was outside and unlit, so in winter going to the toilet was not a pleasant experience, with the cold, cobwebs and spiders. Toilet paper was made from squares of newspaper that had been laboriously torn up and threaded onto a string and hung from a nail on the wooden door. Coal was delivered to the cellar halfway along the hall. The coalman would just come into the house through the unlocked door and deliver the coal, picking up his payment on the way out that had been left at the bottom of the stairs.

My granny died in 1963 aged 88 and the street was demolished in the late 60s. London Street held many fond memories for our family and it was very sad to see it go.

Marilyn Baker

London Street in 1967 showing the advancing threat of demolition.
On the right is the City of London pub with the newly built New England House looming over the doomed area

New Houses on the Block - The Prefabs

Much of the area depicted on early maps as North Butts and The Crook (St. Peter's Place to Viaduct Road) was fully developed by the 1860s. It would be over 80 years before any new housing would to be built, albeit after some tragic circumstances.

On Monday 12th October 1942, an air raid by four German bombers resulted in a line of bombs being dropped in Buckingham Place, Bath Street and Compton Avenue, across to Howard Place, Elder Place (behind Lloyds Bank Preston Circus) and finally onto 64-67 Rose Hill Terrace. The last bomb destroyed all three houses, and severely damaged houses on the north side of the terrace, from the twitten by the London Arms pub (now Viaduct Lane) up to 44 Rose Hill Terrace (now called Rose Hill Close). Despite the raid occurring at lunchtime, only nine people were killed including Edith Orme of 63 Rose Hill Terrace. However, about 100 people were injured and 250 houses damaged.

In 1944, under the recently passed Temporary Housing Act, Brighton shared in the £150m set aside by the Government for the design and production of emergency prefabricated housing, intended to benefit those who had been bombed out of their homes and in anticipation of the post war housing shortage.

The new prefabricated bungalows, 'prefabs' for short, were a vast improvement on previous temporary dwellings, and were in many cases, better than the Victorian housing that they replaced. In 1944 Brighton Corporation took delivery of the first twelve kits of houses destined for the town comprising of 2000 factory-built sections, and they were erected on the Rose Hill Terrace bomb site, and the remains of the gardens of Nos.32-44 Rose Hill Terrace that backed onto Viaduct Road. (There had been no houses on the south side of Viaduct Road, east of No. 32 and the twitten and up to the business premises at 32A). The four prefabs in Viaduct Road were accordingly numbered out of sequence as 32w, 32x, 32y and 32z, thence the business premises started with Field's Decorators as 32a.

The Rose Hill Terrace/Viaduct Road prefabs were built of asbestos, with modern Crittall windows. The roofs were fairly low pitched, and were also made of asbestos covered with bitumen and chippings. The chimneys were of steel, painted black and located just off centre, to the right of each dwelling. The asbestos walls were placed on a brick plinth, with zinc plate as the damp course. Basically, the prefabs were oblong in shape, with a central hallway, at the rear of which was a separate toilet. On the left side of the front door and hallway were two double bedrooms, and at the front on the right of the hallway was the living room. The rear right hand room was divided, with one third of the room accessed from the hallway being the bathroom, with a panelled bath and wash basin unit, and the remaining two thirds, accessed from the living room was the kitchen, which also contained a back door onto the garden. Each prefab came with, a fitted kitchen, a larder, a butler sink with built in cupboards and draining board, a fridge and space for an electric washing copper. The bedrooms had fitted wardrobes, with a further fitted cupboard in the living room.

For temporary housing, expected to last no more than ten years, the prefabs were remarkably well planned and modern for a wartime design of 1944. After these prefabs were erected, others followed on bombsites and on pre-war house clearances. As Britain recovered from the war, the prefabs were gradually replaced, leaving those erected first at Viaduct Road/Rose Hill Terrace as the last to survive. Tenants were moved out of these

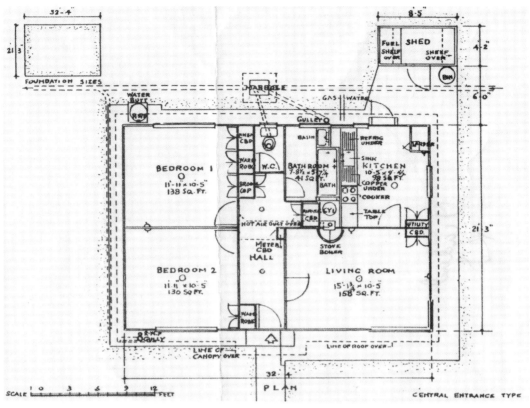

The plan of new prefabs erected on the Rose Hill Terrace bomb site in 1944
It is now the site of Rose Hill Court

Erected in 1944 on the gardens of Nos. 32-44 Rose Hill Terrace,
they were the first prefabs to be erected in Brighton and the last to bc demolished

around 1963/64, but they remained as temporary accommodation for the homeless until 1966, when they were demolished and the site left as a temporary car park for London Road shops. With the building of the York Hill/London Road car park in the mid 1970s, the Viaduct Road site was eventually scheduled for sheltered housing, and Rose Hill Court was built in the early1980s.

My childhood was spent at 32z Viaduct Road, where the family moved in 1951 to be closer to my father's work. Whilst I had a happy childhood, I suffered badly as a chronic asthmatic. My GP expressed concern at my living in a prefab, because of the low structure, which meant that I would be living close to damp and polluted air particularly in winter when coal fires were all alight, and because of the asbestos walls. The novel warm air heating system didn't help my chest: air in a chamber around the chimney stack was supposed to warm up and rise into a duct system which went through to the bedrooms and hallway. But the flue was not that airtight and warm air that circulated was more often than not very smoky, making me wheeze even on a good day. My father rapidly sealed these vents.

By the 1960s the prefabs were in a bad way, the council having done no repairs to them for several years because of their temporary nature. My father was reprimanded by a housing official for buying his own paint to repaint the external doors and window frames, because it was claimed that he was showing how badly the others were in need of attention. It was shortly after that incident that my parents complained so loudly about conditions that they were eventually given a flat in Maple House, Sylvan Hall.

One final memory of the prefabs was the occasion when as a small boy, home sick because of my asthma, I heard a loud noise on the roof. A trolleybus had come around the corner from Ditchling Road too fast, braked suddenly causing the trolley boom to come off the wire. The boom struck the lamp standard and the end of the boom snapped and landed on our roof. The conductor climbed on the roof to retrieve the end of the boom and awaited the repair truck!

Christopher Tullett

The Future

London Road today is typical of many other 21st century busy inner city street with its interesting social and ethnic mix, its combination of multiples and family firms. Like all its counterparts across the country it has a rich, unacknowledged and largely unrecorded history that deserves to be better understood. It has changed greatly over the last two hundred years, from arable fields to smart middle class suburb, from small traders to interwar multiples to 21st century charity shops, fast food and ethnic grocers.

Some elements of the past weave their way through to the present, road names and building lines, building dates and property usage. One aspect of the road is the marked difference between the opposite sides of the highway; the east has seen major rebuilding but on the west there is still a line of handsome 1820s buildings south of Ann Street and north of it are some good 19th century structures.

At the time of writing parts of the area are undergoing change. The future of the Open Market is under discussion. A scheme has been put forward for a continental-style covered market which would have a large central square surrounded by 50 permanent stalls and a gallery with workshops. The market would cover part of Francis Street and in addition on the south side there would be 40 homes.

To the west, the New England Quarter, derelict for over 30 years, has now been re-developed with a new Sainsbury's store and flats. City Point, advertised as an exciting development with 25 two and three-bedroomed apartments has been described as a stunning landmark scheme. Others have expressed different views.

Preston Circus too may also see major changes. The Fire Station is under threat of demolition as it is now considered too small for its present use. There are plans to sell it to make way for a £4 million development. There is strong opposition against the move.

In 2009 a proposal was put forward by St. James Investment to revitalise the London Road area. This included a huge Tesco Store between York Hill and New England Road, demolition of the whole site, the building of a car park for 1,000 cars and tall buildings to replace the workshops and small businesses. After a concerted effort by the action group Another London Road, Tesco announced that it was no longer interested in the site.

Local businesses, dismayed at the decline in the area have formed the London Road Trader's Association to demand that Brighton & Hove City Council and Sussex Police take action to improve the area which has become run down. They want more done to enhance the locality for the benefit of residents and shoppers.

In June 2009, as part of a public consultation, Brighton & Hove City Council held an exhibition in the old Co-op building and welcomed comments and suggestions from the public. We have yet to learn of the council's final vision for the future of London Road.

Bibliography

Roberts, David. A failed rehousing scheme in Brighton by the LBSCR, Sussex Archaeological Society, Lewes Vol. 144 (2006)

Tullett, Christopher. St. Bartholomew's Parish History, (1999).

Carder, Tim. The Encyclopaedia of Brighton, East Sussex County Libraries (1990).

Loudon, John Claudius. Gardener's Magazine, London: Brown, Green & Longman, (1838, 1842).

Loudon, Jane Webb. The Ladies' Flower Garden of Ornamental Annuals, London: William Smith, (1842).

Loudon, Jane Webb. The Ladies' Flower Garden of Ornamental Perennials, London: William Smith, (1844).

Elleray, D. Robert, A Refuge from Reality – The Cinemas of Brighton & Hove: Olio Books (1989)

Hickman, Michael R. A Story to Tell: 200 Years of Methodism in Brighton & Hove: Brighton & Hove Methodist Circuit, (2007).

Banier, Berni. Into the Streets and Lanes. A History of the Brighton & Hove Town Mission 1849-1989: Brighton Town Mission, (1989).

Sources

Mr. B. Mcfarlane - Former Borough Surveyor's Office.

Duke of York's Picture House website.

mybrightonandhove website.

Robert Stuart Nemeth.

East Sussex Record Office – Maps & research.

Brighton History Centre – Research, Rate Books, Electoral Rolls, Census returns. 1841-1911 and Street Directories 1784-1974.

Newspapers - Brighton & Hove Herald and The Brighton Argus & Gazette

Jane Webb Loudon's illustrations are reproduced with the kind permission of the Director and the Board of Trustees, Royal Botanic Gardens, Kew.

Inside back cover:

This small Regency Villa, at 87 London Road, was probably designed by Busby and built by the Wilds c1825. For many years it was the home of the Vicar of Brighton and became the vicarage of St. Bartholomew's church before its conversion to flats

Numbers 54-57 London Road in 2010. Above the shop fronts, the attractive facades give us a glimpse of the original houses before conversion c1900. The Branch Tavern on the left of York Hill opened in the 1830s

Acknowledgements

This publication has been sponsored by:

THE HEDGECOCK BEQUEST and GRASSROOTS

This book was compiled by the London Road Social History Group

Members:

Rosemary Fittock, Geoff Mead, William Parker, Jacqueline Pollard, Jenn Price, Christopher Tullett, Marigold Rogers and Sian Williams.

Contributors:

Eric Nicholls, Doris Vaughan, Sylvia Everett, Ernest Whittington, Sheila Parsley, Pearl Lawrence, Janice Tilley, Barry Leahy, David Guildford, Norman Buxton, Marie Benfield, Beryl Tucknott, Thelma Dove, Dorothy Attrill, Gordon Dean, Paul Moy, Margaret Stewart, David & Carol Drew Bear, David Huggins, Eva Le Grice, Peter Champion, Susan Hill nee Champion, Peter Coombs, Mrs G. Payne, Frank Edwards, Marilyn Baker, Hilda Barber, Stanley Wilson, Peggy Turpin, Peter Llewellyn, Michael Hickman, Mr. A. Elms, Christopher Tullett & Dennis & Marjorie Andrews.

Photographs:

Vanessa Sykes, Peter Booth, Chris Horlock, Vera Brough, Elaine Smith, Jacqueline Pollard, Gill Taylor, Sian Williams, Beryl Tucknott, Frank Edwards, Brenda Roles, Eve Rawley, Margaret Stewart, Brian Page, Marion Devoy, Joan Attwater and Robert Jeeves of 'Step Back in Time' Queen's Road, Brighton, BN1 3WB.

Desk Top Publishing: mac iD, 441 Baltic Chambers, 50 Wellington St. Glasgow G2 6HJ

Printed by Delta Press: Industrial House, Conway Street, Hove BN3 3LW.

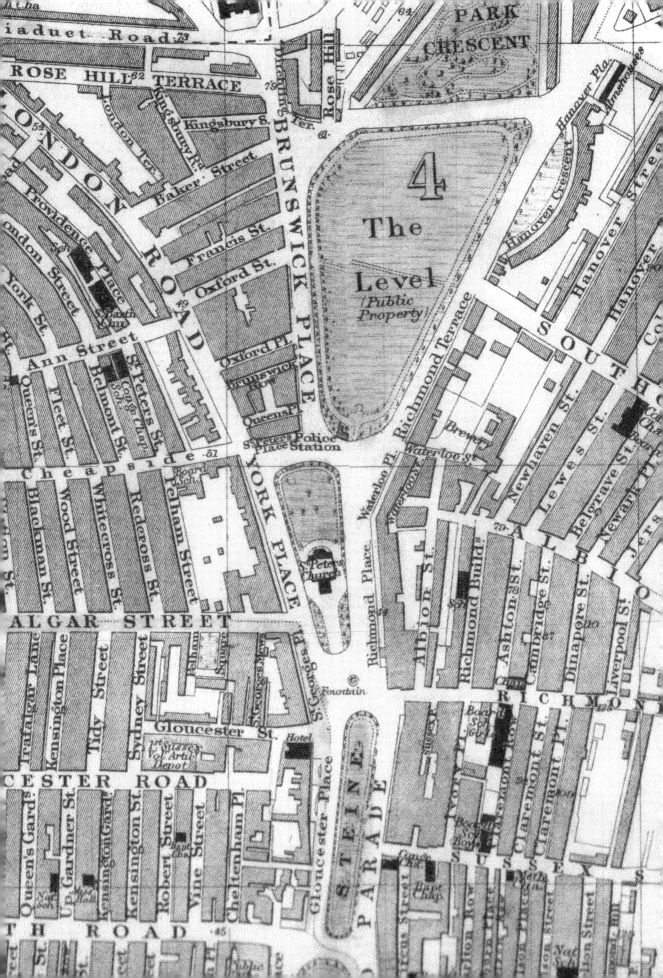

London Road looking north to Preston Circus c1910

CUTRESS BAKERS SHOP - 23 LONDON STREET.
Edward Cutress & family outside their baker's shop at 23 London Street c1885, his son Edward proudly posing
with his penny-farthing bicycle. The Cutress family moved from London Street in the 1890s,
although it remained a baker's shop until 1939. London Street was demolished in the late 1960s.

Previous Page: New Ordnance Survey Map of Brighton 1882

23 ST. PETER'S STREET
Pat & Frank Carver stand outside their home at 23 St. Peter's Street (west side) c1928.
The street was built c1842 and demolished in the 1960s.

Elder Row in June 1955 ran from York Hill to New England Road. It faced the backs of the Elder Street houses and was demolished in 1958. The name Elder comes from the Elder trees once grown in this area.
The site is now dominated by New England House.

Inside front cover: Plan of the Parish of Brighthelmstone 1792
showing the field patterns of the London Road area